Natural Adventures in the Mountains of North Georgia

Mary Ellen Hammond
and Jim Parham

milestone press

almond, nc

Milestone Press, P.O. Box 158, Almond, NC 28702
http://www.milestonepress.com

Book design and drawings by Ron Roman/Treehouse Communications
Photos (except as indicated) by Mary Ellen Hammond
Copy editing by Gene Smith/Articulate INK

Printed in the United States on recycled paper.

For Miriam Powell Parham and F.T."Pete" Parham,
whose love of natural adventures
in the outdoors has been an inspiration.

Contents

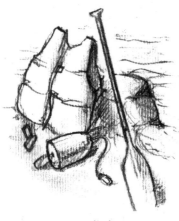

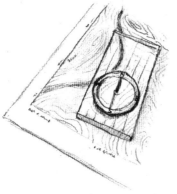

Introduction

As you travel north from Atlanta into the mountains of Georgia, one of the first things you'll notice is that everything begins to slow down. Traffic, even on the major highways, moves along at a more leisurely pace; you'll swear the people talk slower; and you may even notice you've slowed down as well. The north Georgia mountains have a calming effect on folks, and maybe that's one reason people love to vacation and live here.

Another thing you can't help noticing is the incredible scenery. Mountains rise up and envelop you almost before you realize it. All around are splashing streams, green trees, and flowers in bloom. Get out of the car and you'll hear birds calling. You may spot a deer, a turkey, or, more commonly, a squirrel. If it's summertime, you'll also notice it's somewhat cooler than the regions to the south.

The "natural adventures" in this book involve nature or the great outdoors. They can be learning experiences—ones that stretch the mind or body—or simply great times, on your own or with friends or family.

ADVENTURE FOR EVERYONE

Here, as anywhere, adventure is in the eye of the beholder. You'll find some of the activities we list involve an element of risk, but the majority require only that you exert yourself to the point where your body feels rejuvenated by mountain air and sunlight. For some people, an adventure simply could be driving along a scenic byway and stopping to get out and stretch their legs while they soak in the view. For others, it's a rugged overnight hike on the Appalachian Trail. For still others, it might be a day of historical exploration at one of the Civil War battlefields, learning about and tasting old Southern apples, or enjoying old-timey music at an outdoor festival. Our intention here is to help you sort through the opportunities available in this region and to open your eyes to the best natural adventures at hand. We list 52 in all, and these should spark ideas and interest for many more.

VARIETY IS THE SPICE OF THESE MOUNTAINS

It seems only fitting that we begin the book with a section called *Back to Nature*. We think of nature as the natural scenery, including the wild plants and animals that are part of it. In this section, the activities will help you get in tune with your surroundings. Next, *Outdoor Activities* will put you out on the trail and into camp. *Watersports* like whitewater rafting and tubing follow. And if sightseeing from the car is more to your liking, look to the *Auto Touring* section. Some of the best views around are seen from the roadways that pave the way to remarkable destinations.

North Georgia's *Natural Wonders*, including its two canyons and a wild & scenic river, are followed by *Native American History*.

For long before European explorers arrived, Native American tribes lived on the land. You can follow their story from the mounds at Etowah to the Cherokee "Trail of Tears." Major battles of the American Civil War were fought in the north Georgia mountains, and the *Civil War History* section is a must for any adventurous traveler.

Finally, we leave you with a few of the region's natural attractions that are classics. We think these *Classic Attractions* are ones you won't want to miss.

INFORMATION TO HELP YOU PLAN YOUR TRIP

Each entry in this book presents information on a two-page spread. On the left is a short description of the activity, including the location; a map and directions if relevant; dates of operation if the attraction is seasonal; prices if there is a cost involved; and suggestions for what to bring. Special notes highlight nearby activities or other specific points, and a listing of available facilities such as restrooms, telephones, or handicapped access is given as well.

The right-hand page provides history, tips, anecdotes, or facts relevant to the activity or destination. It's worth reading these pages in advance of your visit. Last, but not least, check out the appendix. It contains a wealth of details to assist you in planning. Look here for everything from suggested day hikes to a list of addresses, phone numbers, and web sites for outdoor outfitters.

We suggest you flip through the book and find adventures suited to your time frame, your fancy, and your pocketbook. In many cases, several different activities or points of interest are located close enough to each other to be combined for a half day or even a full day of adventuring. But don't overdo it! You'll find it more satisfying to choose just a few and really enjoy them than to run yourself ragged sprinting from one place to another.

SPEND A DAY, OR AN ENTIRE VACATION

Natural adventuring in the north Georgia mountains is a great way to spend a day, a weekend, or an entire series of vacations. Whether you live a thousand miles away or right in the heart of the Georgia mountains themselves, you'll find activities here you can enjoy time and time again. We want you to really use this book—make notes in it, wear it out. That way, you'll make these adventures your own.

M.E.H. & J.P.
March 2000

Back to Nature

In a book of natural adventures, it may seem redundant to title a section "Back to Nature." But in north Georgia there are so many activities that fall under the "natural" heading, we sometimes have to be reminded about some of the most simple and pleasing of them.

EACH SEASON OFFERS DIFFERENT DELIGHTS

In this region, spring is heralded with the most brilliant of floral displays—from early April when pristine dogwood blooms frost the woods, to the deep purple ironweed and bright goldenrod that grace the fields in fall. You can find some of the most beautiful flowers along north Georgia's many nature trails—or perhaps you'll prefer just a quiet walk through the woods. In summer, the time is ripe for berry picking along the roadsides or in higher elevations. Autumn is the season for leaf-looking, whether you're on foot carrying a day pack, or touring a beautiful byway by car.

Of course, if you're seeking more in-depth information about the natural world around you, you can find it at places like the Elachee Nature Center, where you'll learn the finer points of composting and conservation. Whatever you choose, you're sure to come away feeling closer to the earth, with a deeper understanding of what it means to call this place home.

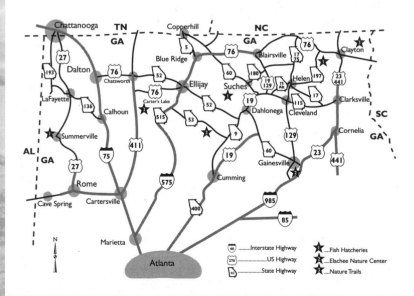

Spotting Wildflowers

The blossoms of the wild dogwood tree are Georgia's state flower.

If the weather is warm in north Georgia, you can bet one thing—something will be blooming. In early spring you'll find perfectly white wild dogwoods, Georgia's state flower. Closer to the ground, look for trillium, violets, lady's slippers, and jack-in-the-pulpits. Later on, in May and June, you'll see mountain laurel and orange flame azaleas dotting the higher elevations. Lush stands of rhododendron bloom along whitewater streams and rivers in June and July. And as autumn arrives, look for Queen Anne's lace, ironweed, and asters scattered in the fields.

LOCATION
Just about anywhere in north Georgia, especially in the Chattahoochee National Forest or in any of the state parks.

SEASON
Late March–October

TIME ALLOWANCE
As long as you like.

COST
Free

BRING ALONG
Camera, hand lens, notebook or log, field guides for wildflowers (see p. 135).

NOTE
One of the most beautiful displays of mountain laurel can be found in May atop Brasstown Bald (p. 80).

Remember—celebrate a wildflower on the stem, not in the hand! It is illegal to pick wildflowers on national forest or state park lands. And before eating any plant, be sure you are absolutely certain you've identified it correctly.

Clusters of delicately scented, dainty mountain laurel blooms appear in May.

SOME WILDFLOWERS OR THEIR ASSOCIATED PLANTS CAN BE CONSUMED

Many wildflowers (or the plants on which the flowers bloom) are edible, and some are even considered delicacies. Below are several easy-to-spot edible flowers, with information from *Eat The Weeds* by Ben Charles Harris (Barre Publishing, 1968) on how they may be prepared.

QUEEN ANNE'S LACE

This tall white flower, also known as *Bird's Nest*, is actually wild carrot (*Daucus carota*). Both its roots and seeds are edible. If the plant is found in rich soil, the root is large and sweet. If it is found in hard or sandy soil, it is small and tastes not nearly so good. Steam it in a little water and add it to soups and stews. The seeds, too, make fine seasoning for soups and stews. You might even try them on baked wild mountain trout.

BEE BALM

Early colonists in America knew this herb *as Oswego*. If you check your history, you'll find that the substitute of choice for China tea following the Boston Tea Party was Oswego tea. To make it, pick the small leaves from the upper half of the plant and add a few petals from the flower, then brew by steeping them in hot water as you would any other tea.

Edible Flowers

STAGHORN SUMAC

This easily identifiable plant can be used to make a cool tasty drink. Grind up a teaspoonful of either berries or flower petals and steep in a covered cup of hot water for 5–6 minutes. Strain and then cool in the refrigerator or pour over ice. You may even want to sweeten it with a little sourwood honey. Enjoy!

VIOLETS (BIRDSFOOT, LONGSPUR, SWEET WHITE)

Violets have a variety of uses. Medicinally, the leaves and flower petals are useful for their emollient and expectorant properties in treating bouts of bronchitis. Use the young leaves to thicken soups and stews. The leaves are mucilaginous—in fact, one variety is known as wild okra. Lastly, by "sugaring" the flowers, bakers use them as a lovely decoration for cakes.

Following the Boston Tea Party in 1773, bee balm provided the substitute drink of choice.

Nature Trails

Nature trails let you take the time to really look at the natural world.

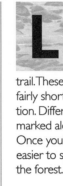

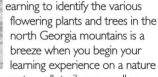

Learning to identify the various flowering plants and trees in the north Georgia mountains is a breeze when you begin your learning experience on a nature trail. These easy-to-walk trails are usually fairly short and contain a wealth of information. Different flowers, plants, and trees are marked along the way for easy identification. Once you've seen them on the trail, they are easier to spot you are when out and about in the forest.

LOCATIONS
• **Georgia State Parks**
• **Chattahoochee National Forest**
• **Elachee Nature Center** (p. 20)
• **Carter's Lake**
See p. 131 for details and directions.

SEASON
Year-round

TIME ALLOWANCE
1–1½ hours

COST
Free

BRING ALONG
Hiking shoes, water bottle, camera, binoculars, clothes for the season plus an extra layer, rain gear, and perhaps a magnifying glass.

NATURE LOVERS OF TODAY GIVE THANKS TO ARTHUR WOODY

Once you've visited a few of north Georgia's nature trails, you'll find yourself going about the woods spotting the plants and animals you've learned to identify. Fortunately for us, there are plenty of wild lands protected from development left to explore in these mountains. If there were any one individual deserving the most thanks for this, it would be Arthur Woody.

NORTH GEORGIA'S FIRST FOREST RANGER

Born in Suches on April 1, 1884, Arthur Woody has the distinction of being north Georgia's first national

This Arthur Woody mannequin tells stories daily at the interpretive center atop Brasstown Bald.

A Man Who Preserved and Restored Nature

forest ranger. His father is said to have shot the last deer in the Georgia mountains. You read it right—at the turn of the century, there were no deer left. During Woody's years as a ranger, he traveled far and wide, buying and trapping deer to bring back to the mountains. By 1941 there were enough deer for the state to reopen a deer hunting season.

BUYING UP THE WASTELAND AND RESTORING THE FOREST

Along with bringing back the deer, Woody is credited with buying for the US government most of the land that is now the Chattahoochee National Forest. In the early 1900s much of the forested land we now enjoy was overlogged and barren, stripped by the lumber companies. These folks were too busy to replant the trees, and the land left behind was considered worthless. Woody would go in, buy parcels of land, and then sell it to the Forest Service. In the 1930s the forest was replanted by the Civilian Conservation Corps. The wildlife, scenic vistas, and nature hikes we enjoy today in north Georgia might have been very different had it not been for Arthur Woody. He died in Suches on June 10, 1946.

Observing Wildlife

One of the best places to see deer is in the fields at Berry College.

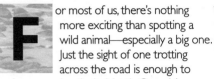

For most of us, there's nothing more exciting than spotting a wild animal—especially a big one. Just the sight of one trotting across the road is enough to make your spine tingle. North Georgia's mountains and forests are full of all sorts of wildlife. You may see deer, bear, foxes, ground hogs, grouse, pileated woodpeckers, and others. Consider keeping a running log of the different animals you see, how many, and where. Children especially enjoy finding out who can catch sight of the largest, most unusual, and most colorful animals. Right here is a great place to begin.

LOCATION
Almost anywhere, but the some of the best places to see deer are the fields at Berry College and Chickamauga National Battlefield Park. For smaller species, nature trails offer an excellent place for viewing.

SEASON
Year-round

TIME ALLOWANCE
As long as you like.

COST
Free

BRING ALONG
Camera; binoculars; notebook or log; field guides for birds, mammals, amphibians, etc.

NOTE
The best time of day to spot larger mammals is just after sunrise and just before sunset when they come out to feed. **Remember: never feed any wild animal.**

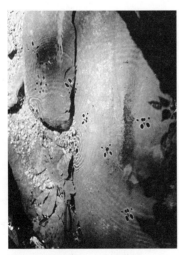

These waterbugs are visible because of their shadows on the streambed.

Predator Calling

PREDATORS ARE THE MOST WARY OF ALL ANIMALS

It's true that you have to go where the animals are to see the animals. But it doesn't hurt to stack the deck a little every now and then. One way of doing this is by using a predator call. Predators are the most wary of all animals. They include bobcats, foxes, hawks, eagles—even bears—and it is rare indeed to just happen upon one in the wild. A predator call makes the sound of a wounded rabbit and can be purchased relatively inexpensively from a sporting goods store. With it, you can attempt to draw these animals to you.

How to use a predator call is well known, but the best description of the technique appears in Joseph Cornell's *Sharing Nature With Children* (Dawn Publications, 1979), which we highly recommend and from which the following is adapted.

PICK YOUR SPOT CAREFULLY

With your predator call in hand, walk quietly into the woods and find a place with signs of animal activity, such as a game trail or watering hole. Next, arrange yourself in a thicket with a good view of an open area or clearing. You want your relationship to the clearing to be such that you can see the predator long before it sees you.

IMPERSONATING A WOUNDED RABBIT

Now it's time to try out your call. Most come with instructions, and you can also purchase tapes of the sounds you will want to make. Basically, you want to coax from the instrument a wail that is similar to a human baby's cry. Repeat this wail a few times loudly and then reduce it to a whimper. Practicing ahead of time will increase the chances of it sounding as realistic as possible.

THE RESULTS CAN BE SPECTACULAR

You won't attract a predator every time you use your call, but when you do, the results can be spectacular. Remember, you are what a predator thinks is an injured animal. Until you let it be known otherwise, that predator may think you're its next meal! At any moment a fox or bobcat or hawk could be circling in for the kill. You may even draw the attention of some non-predators. Nearby deer may walk over to have a look. When you've had enough calling, or some animal is getting a little too close for comfort, let your true identity be known.

State Fish Hatcheries

The rivers and creeks of north Georgia are famous for an abundance of trout and other fish, and the reason why can be found at the state fish hatcheries. At these state-supported hatcheries, fish are raised in simulated streams. When they reach an appropriate size, they are deposited in many of the region's creeks and rivers, where anglers lure them with hand-tied flies. If it happens to be feeding time at the hatchery, you'll get to witness a real, live feeding frenzy. The water is so clear you'll see hundreds of fish wrestling for the food.

The Chattahoochee Hatchery produces trout for Georgia's mountain streams.

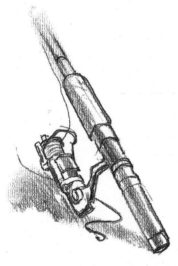

LOCATION
- **Lake Burton Hatchery** on GA 197 adjacent to Moccasin Creek State Park.
- **Chattahoochee National Forest Fish Hatchery** located on FS 69 south of GA 60 between Suches and Blue Ridge.
- **Summerville Hatchery** on Fish Hatchery Road just west of Summerville off GA 48.

SEASON
Year-round
Daily, 8 am – 5 pm

TIME ALLOWANCE
½–1 hour

COST
Free

BRING ALONG
Camera, picnic.

NOTE
Many people like to fish the stream adjacent to the Chattahoochee National Forest Fish Hatchery, and children and seniors can trout fish for free in the stream adjacent to the Lake Burton Hatchery. Camping is nearby to both.

Restrooms
Picnic Tables
Handicapped Access

FIRST, YOU'VE GOT TO HAVE A FISHING LICENSE

Persons over the age of 16 wishing to fish in the state of Georgia must first obtain a fishing license. These licenses can be purchased three different ways: at most sporting goods stores, bait & tackle shops, marinas, and hardware stores; by telephone at 800-748-6887; or over the Internet at www.permit.com. In addition to the regular fishing license, if you want to fish for trout and are between the ages of 16 and 65, a special trout license must also be purchased. *If you are a nonresident and want to fish for trout, you must purchase both a fishing license and a trout license regardless of your age or physical condition.*

Lakes and streams are stocked from hatcheries so families can enjoy moments like this.

Georgia Fishing Regulations

LICENSE FEES

Resident Licenses:

Yearly fishing	$9.00
One-day fishing	$3.50
Trout	$5.00

Nonresident Licenses:

Season fishing	$24.00
Seven-day fishing	$7.00
One-day fishing	$3.50
Trout	$13.00

YOU CAN ONLY KEEP SO MANY FISH

Creel limits are set for different species of fish:

Bass	10
Crappie	30
Pickerel	15
Sauger	8
Shad	8
Sunfish or Bream	50
Trout	8
Walleye	8

FISH FOR FREE

If you are a Georgia resident, you can fish for free three days out of the year—two in June and one in September. Call 770-918-6400 or find www.ganet.org/dnr/wild/ on the Web for details.

Wild Berry Pickin'

Blackberries are so abundant in north Georgia you'd swear they grow on the pine trees too!

Wild blueberry cobbler, fresh blackberries on breakfast cereal, just-turned homemade huckleberry ice cream … yum! With a little effort these scrumptious, palate-pleasing delicacies can be yours. In fact, they're just a hand's reach away. Berries abound in the mountains in summertime, and there's nothing more rewarding than picking a pail or two for the table.

LOCATION
The best place to pick wild huckleberries or blueberries is along the trails in the higher elevations of the state. Blackberries are found in valley fields, in timbercuts, and alongside roadways.

SEASON
Mid- to late July

TIME ALLOWANCE
You'll need to pick for at least an hour to get any quantity at all.

COST
Free

BRING ALONG
Picking pails (*milk jugs work well—cut them off at the top and attach them to your waist by running your belt through the handle*), water, sun protection, snacks, picnic.

NOTE
Never venture onto private land to pick without permission.

What you wear makes a difference—for blackberries, wear a hat and cover up well.

BERRY PICKING IS MORE FUN IF YOU'RE PREPARED

Before you head out the door on that berry picking trip it will pay you to do a little planning ahead. First, consider your clothing. Blackberries require something just shy of full body armor. Plan to wear boots or sturdy shoes, long pants, a long sleeved shirt, and a hat to protect you from thorns, chiggers, and the sun. Make sure your duds are fairly durable; cotton fabric tends to work better than synthetics. Wearing so much clothing, you will want to pick early in the day when it's cooler.

For blueberries or huckleberries, you'll want to cut back on the amount of clothing you wear. A sun hat, sturdy shoes, short sleeved shirt, and even shorts will do.

TOOLS OF THE TRADE

Tools are few, but one is essential to a successful picking experience. Find a gallon-sized plastic milk or water

Ready, Set, Pick ...

jug. Take a knife or scissors and cut off the top while leaving the handle intact (see *illustration*). This will be your picking bucket. Run a belt other than the one holding up your pants or a length of rope through the jug handle and then secure it around your waist. A pail with a handle will also work, but the gallon container gives you a better idea of just how many berries you've picked. The container and your free hands are all the tools you'll need.

HERE'S A REAL TREAT

FRESH BLUEBERRY OR BLACKBERRY COBBLER

½ cup butter or margarine, softened
½ cup sugar
1 cup unbleached white flour
⅛ teaspoon nutmeg
1 teaspoon orange rind, grated
3 cups fresh wild berries

Preheat the oven to 375°. combine the sugar and flour in a bowl, then cut in the butter with a fork until the mixture is uniformly crumbly. Add the orange rind and nutmeg and toss. Pour the berries into an 8- or 9-inch baking dish. Sprinkle the topping over the berries and bake for 30 minutes or until the topping is golden brown.

Try serving this cobbler with vanilla ice cream!

Elachee Nature Center

Ever looked through a window inside a tree? You can at Elachee.

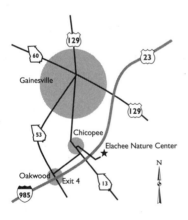

Restrooms
Picnic Tables
Handicapped Access

esigned with learning in mind, the Elachee Nature Center makes for a great outing. It is especially suitable for children and caters to groups and individuals alike. The museum contains two hands-on exhibit halls and a live animal room. You can learn about natural habitats, recycling, solutions to pollution, and more. There are also a number of trails through various outdoor ecosystems. In addition, a network of mountain biking trails runs through the complex.

LOCATION
2125 Elachee Drive, Gainesville GA 30504. Take Exit 4 from I-985 and follow signs to the center.
770-535-1976
www.elachee.net

SEASON
Year-round
Monday–Saturday, 10 am – 5 pm
Closed on major holidays.

TIME ALLOWANCE
2–4 hours

COST RANGE:
Adults: $3.00
Children 2–12: $1.50

BRING ALONG
Camera, walking shoes, questions.

NOTE
Elachee Nature Center is accredited as a Supplementary Education School and offers a vast assortment of outdoor classroom sessions. Classes last anywhere from two hours to all day and are appropriate from preschool to high school level students.

COMPOSTING:
IT'S NOT A NEW IDEA

The concept of composting has been around for quite a long time. The first written record of it appears in about 2300 BC. Homer wrote about it in *The Odyssey*, and the Romans experimented widely with composting, using a variety of materials. Today, we compost many things in many different ways: Farmers compost manure. Gardeners compost kitchen scraps, leaves, and yard clippings. Municipalities compost organic material in garbage.

WHAT *IS* COMPOST, ANYWAY?

Compost is actually a humus-rich soil derived from the natural breakdown of organic materials. Finished compost looks and smells like dirt. Humus is a dark brown, porous, spongy, somewhat gummy, and pleasantly earthy smelling substance. Added to garden soil, it increases the amount of air and water available to plants, releases nutrients as plants need them, and promotes resistance to diseases and insect pests.

YOU CAN COMPOST, TOO

Composting is easy, and it's something you can feel good about doing. First, you must decide if you want to take the fast approach (hot composting) or the slow, kick-back-and-relax approach (cold composting). Hot composting requires quite a bit of attention and no small amount of work, but you

Composting

can end up with finished compost in as little as three weeks. The cold method may take as long as a year, but the work involved is minimal.

COMPOSTING BASICS

Whether you compost hot or cold, you'll need a place to pile your materials. You can build elaborate bin systems, purchase various sized composters, dig a pit, or just throw your waste in a heap. You can even compost indoors in small containers. There are many different recipes

for mixing your compost, but basically you will need about equal amounts of "browns" (carbon-rich dry materials like dead leaves, straw, shredded newspaper, eggshells) and "greens" (nitrogen-rich wet things like grass clippings, kitchen scraps, coffee grounds, farm manure). Avoid adding meat or dairy products, which attract pests, or anything with chemicals added. Keep at it and before you know it, you'll have a beautiful pile of rich compost.

Quiet Walks

Most children will jump at the opportunity to go for a walk.

Sometimes there is no better refresher than a quiet walk in the woods. Scattered throughout the mountains are trails of all sorts, and many are easily accessible from roadside pull-offs. When you've had enough of being in the car, a short walk on a trail can calm your nerves and renew your spirits.

It doesn't really matter where you choose to walk as long as it is not on posted private land. The object is to get out and stretch your legs, escape the sounds of traffic, and breathe in fresh air. So if things are getting a bit hectic in the car, pull over and give everyone a break. You'll be glad you did.

LOCATION
Almost anywhere. Along the roadsides, out from your lodging or campground, beside a picnic area, along a stream—the choice is yours.

SEASON
Year-round

TIME ALLOWANCE
10 minutes to ½ hour

COST
Free

BRING ALONG
Camera, walking shoes, binoculars.

NOTE
You really don't *need* anything special for the walk, not even walking shoes. The idea is to take a break from the mechanical world of autos and noise, and experience the quiet natural surroundings firsthand.

ON A QUIET WALK, TRY A QUIET SIT

The art of still hunting has been practiced for centuries, and for most of that time the goal has been to put meat on the table. In this variation of the still hunt, the idea is to see as much wildlife as possible by sitting very quietly and observing all that comes into your range of vision.

PICK YOUR SPOT AND HAVE A SEAT

Begin your still hunt by walking quietly into the forest. It does not really matter how far you go in, but make it at least far enough that you have woods all around you. Now pick a spot that looks as if it might be a comfortable place to sit for a while. It could be at the base of a big tree, on a log, or atop a boulder. Try also to pick a place that gives you a good view of the surrounding woods.

SIT AS STILL AND AS QUIETLY AS POSSIBLE

Now take a seat and get comfortable. You'll probably rustle around at first, but try to settle in and sit as quietly and as still as possible. Look with your eyes, not with your head

Still Hunting

Who knows what you'll see as you sit in your spot.

and body. As you sit there, the woods will seem pretty quiet at first, but slowly you'll start to hear more and more sounds closer and closer to you. Resist the impulse to jerk around and look in the direction of every sound. Give the forest time to gradually come back to life and accept your presence. It may take 10, 15, or 20 minutes—rarely more.

ONCE YOU'RE ACCEPTED, YOU CAN RELAX AND ENJOY THE SHOW

After this "break in" period, you'll find that the creatures of the forest have accepted your presence and are now going about their daily routines. You'll also find you can look around a bit more and even scratch those terminal itches without startling any wildlife. This is also when you'll see the most activity. Keep quiet and stay as long as you like. Who knows what will come walking into view!

Autumn Foliage

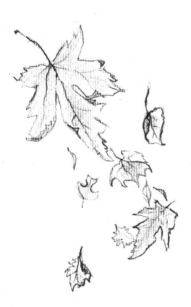

Sunshine and crisp weather bring out the best leaf colors.

O utside the South, the glorious fall colors of the north Georgia mountains are a well kept secret. Spring dogwoods are famous for their blooms, and oak and hickory provide cooling summer shade. But at no other time of year do trees command our attention here as they do in autumn, when brilliant leaves blaze against clear blue skies. Whether you're in a car, on foot, or tubing a mountain stream, it's well worth the trip to see the spectacle. October is one of the busiest tourist months of the year in this region. But even if you can't abide crowds, with a little perseverance you can almost always find a quiet spot along a creek or atop a windy bald to enjoy Mother Nature's brilliant swan song as she surrenders to winter's imminent arrival.

LOCATION

Leaves in the higher elevations change color first, so head for **Brasstown Bald**, the **Russell/ Brasstown Scenic Byway**, **Cloudland Canyon**, or any of the high elevation dirt roads. As the season progresses, the color moves down the mountains.

SEASON

Late September – early November

TIME ALLOWANCE

As long as you like.

COST

Free

BRING ALONG

Camera, binoculars, sweater, rain jacket, leaf or fall color guide.

NOTE

Mix leaf-looking with other activities like day hikes (p. 28), auto touring (p. 55), the natural wonders (p. 79), or a raft trip (p. 44).

How Autumn Leaves Change Color

CHLOROPHYLLS MAKE THE LEAVES GREEN

A green leaf is green because of the presence of a group of pigments known as *chlorophylls*. During the growing season, the chlorophylls' green color dominates, masking out the colors of any other pigments, thus the leaves of summer are characteristically green.

Chlorophylls are vital to the plant because they capture energy from the sun and use it to manufacture food—simple sugars produced from water and carbon dioxide. Although chlorophylls are used up in the food manufacturing process, during the growing season they are replenished by the plant, so the supply remains high and leaves stay green.

CAROTENOIDS GIVE US YELLOWS, ORANGES, AND BROWNS

As autumn approaches and the days grow shorter, the chlorophylls break down more quickly than they are replaced. During this period, with the total supply of chlorophylls gradually dwindling, the "masking" effect slowly fades away. Other pigments that have been present in the cells all during the leaf's life begin to show through. These are the *carotenoids*, which give us colorations of yellow, brown, and orange.

Carotenoids are common in many living things, giving characteristic color to carrots, corn, and canaries, as well as egg yolks, buttercups, and bananas. In the north Georgia mountains' autumn forest, their brilliant yellows and oranges are seen in hardwood species such as hickory, ash, maple, poplar, birch, black cherry, sycamore, and sassafras.

ANTHOCYANINS GIVE US REDS AND PURPLES

The reds, purples, and blended combinations of the two that decorate autumn foliage come from yet another group of pigments called *anthocyanins*. Unlike the carotenoids, which are present in the leaf throughout the growing season, anthocyanins develop in late summer in the sap of the cells of the leaf. Their formation depends on the breakdown of sugars in the presence of bright light as the level of phosphate in the leaf is reduced.

You've seen anthocyanins before, too. They give the familiar color to fruits such as blueberries, cherries, strawberries, and plums. In north Georgia forests, anthocyanins show up vividly in maples, oaks, sourwood, sweet gum, dogwood, black gum, and persimmon. These same pigments often combine with the carotenoids' colors to give us the deeper orange, fiery reds, and bronzes typical of many hardwood species.

Outdoor Activities

Most of the best activities here in the mountains of north Georgia are done out of doors. This section includes the traditional land-based activities for the region. Of these, horseback riding, hiking, camping, picnicking, and trout fishing are the classics. Many trails here date back to the Civilian Conservation Corps of the 1930s, and the old CCC camps have become the public campgrounds and picnic areas of today. Back then, seeing real wilderness meant spending days—and nights—on the trail.

NEW RECREATIONAL OPTIONS

While traditional land-based activities thrive in the mountains of north Georgia, there are some new recreational kids on the block. Mountain biking burst onto the scene in the mid-1980s and now is one of the most popular sports in the woods. North Georgia's paved backroads are excellent for road biking as well. Whichever one you choose, you'll find this region an excellent outdoor destination.

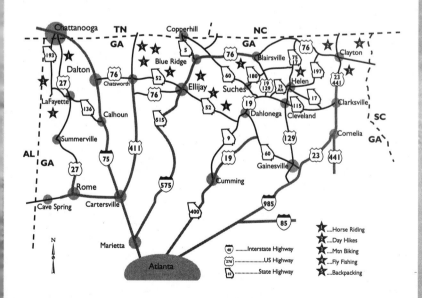

Day Hikes

Be sure to bring plenty of water and take breaks often.

SUGGESTED HIKES

See pp. 136–137 for detailed directions and descriptions.

Springer Mountain/Three Forks
Several loop or out-and-back trails include the Appalachian Trail and the Benton MacKaye Trail.

Blood Mountain/Vogel State Park
Popular hikes along the Appalachian Trail, the Bear Hair Trail, and around Sosebee Cove.

Cloudland Canyon
Trails follow the rim and traverse the canyon.

Black Rock Mountain State Park
A beautiful trail in Georgia's highest state park.

A t one time, the only way to see the north Georgia mountains was on foot. It's still one of the best ways. With hundreds and hundreds of miles of maintained trails inside the Chattahoochee National Forest and within the Georgia state parks, there are plenty to choose from. Many hikes leading to some pretty special places can be done in less than a day. On this page we've made some suggestions to get you started; see the appendix for additional details. You'll enjoy discovering more on your own.

LOCATION
Suggested hikes at left and on pp. 136–137.

SEASON
Year-round

TIME ALLOWANCE
3–4 hours to a full day

COST
Free

BRING ALONG
Hiking attire, maps & guidebooks, water bottle, camera, binoculars, sunscreen, day pack, sweater, rain gear, small first-aid kit.

NOTE
No matter what the season, mountain weather can be unpredictable. Carry suitable clothing and gear. Never assume stream or spring water is drinkable. Be prepared with some method of water purification (iodine tablets, for instance) in case you run out of the water you bring with you.

MAP AND COMPASS SKILLS ARE USEFUL ON THE TRAIL

Ever heard someone say, "Going for a hike? ... Don't forget your map and compass."? This is great advice, provided you actually know how to use a map and compass. Sadly, it may be heard less and less with the growing popularity of GPS (Global Positioning Systems). Still, knowing how to use a topographic map and a compass is a great skill. Here are the most basic of compass basics.

TOPOGRAPHIC MAPS: SNAPSHOTS OF THE LAND

USGS topographic maps may be purchased from outfitters or from the US Forest Service. Maps of the

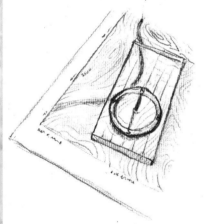

7.5-minute series cover approximately 60 square miles per map. Each one will show every stream, river, or lake, and the contour of the land in 20- or 40-foot increments. This kind of detail tells you exactly

A Simple Lesson in Map & Compass

what the land will look like, but not the thickness of the vegetation you'll encounter on your hike.

IT'S IMPORTANT TO ORIENT YOUR MAP TO YOUR COMPASS

Topographic maps, like most maps, are oriented north. USGS maps have a diagram delineating magnetic north from true north. This difference is called *declination*. The declination for much of north Georgia is 3° or less. It is important when using your map and compass to allow for this difference; an error of 14° means you will stray ¼ mile for every mile you travel.

USING MAP AND COMPASS TOGETHER CAN HELP YOU STAY ON TRACK

Compasses come in all shapes and sizes, but they all have one thing in common: a floating magnetic needle, one end of which always points north (*magnetic* north—see above). Around the needle are a series of hash marks with numbers next to them. Letters denote North, East, South, and West. The hash marks and numbers represent degrees from magnetic north. Competent students of map and compass, finding themselves disoriented, can use these to pinpoint their exact location on the map. They can then decide from the map where they need to go, and use the compass to keep to their courses.

Picnicking

A shady roadside patch of grass can make a good picnic spot.

A picnic can be anything from a convenient impromptu stop on a long trip to a planned family outing. The mountains are full of fantastic picnic areas, from scenic to secluded, and there's always a good one nearby. Remember: a well planned picnic can include games, short hikes, wading or swimming in nearby streams, or wildlife observation.

LOCATION
Most of the recreation areas within the Chattahoochee National Forest have picnic areas, as do the state parks. (see listings pp. 131–135). You also will find picnic tables scattered across the landscape at various road pull-offs.

SEASON
Year-round, but best April–October

TIME ALLOWANCE
2–4 hours

COST
Many are free, but you will find some of the national forest recreation areas now charge a use fee, as do the state parks ($2–3).

BRING ALONG
Food, drinks, tablecloth, charcoal for grilling, frisbee, balls, camera, swimsuit, old shoes for wading, hiking shoes, a trash bag for cleanup.

NOTE
You don't always have to go to a picnic area for a really nice picnic. Pack an old blanket in your car trunk or rucksack and take your spread to a mountaintop meadow, a stream-side rock, or just set up in the grass alongside a scenic byway.

Roadside picnic tables are numerous in the mountains.

THE NEW DEAL AND THE CIVILIAN CONSERVATION CORPS

In 1933, with the United States in the depths of the Great Depression, President Franklin D. Roosevelt developed a plan called The New Deal to help the nation. One part of this New Deal was to put young men across America, mostly from the cities, to work. The program created to do this was called the Civilian Conservation Corps (CCC). Not only did the CCC program create jobs, it played a major role in creating resources for backcountry recreation as we know it today.

BUILDING OUR RECREATIONAL PLAYGROUNDS

Known as "the boys of the CCC," these workers built dams, fought forest fires, planted trees, and constructed trails in the wilderness. Much of the north Georgia forests we know today looked very different in the 1930s. Some had become virtual wastelands, ravaged by excessive logging and the resulting erosion.

For the more than two million men serving in the CCC, there were only so many fires to fight and only so many dams to be built, but there

The "Boys of the CCC"

were millions of seedlings to plant. Many of the trees we take for granted in today's north Georgia forests are the work of the Civilian Conservation Corps. In addition, they built many of the hundreds of miles of trails that crisscross north Georgia—trails that would not exist had the boys of the CCC not played the part they did.

CCC CAMPS OF YESTERYEAR ARE PICNIC AREAS TODAY

CCC workers were divided into groups and shipped out all over the country to do their assigned jobs. These hardy fellows not only worked every day in the forest, they lived there as well. Vast camps were set up in the wilderness to house the men. Living in tents or log structures, they dined, slept, and worked together day by day.

What became of these great camps? Many of them are now our picnic and recreation areas! The CCC was disbanded in 1942 on the eve of World War II, but its legacy lives on. On your next picnic, take a look around. Chances are, you'll find a marker telling the story of the "boys of the CCC" who once worked and lived at the site.

Bicycling

Single-track trails are a mountain biker's dream come true.

n the last decade, the sport of mountain biking has exploded in north Georgia. The most popular areas are at Bull Mountain near Dahlonega and in the Ellijay area. Classic road biking is also popular in this region. For road bikers, many of the lightly-motored paved roads winding through these mountains offer scenic beauty and physical challenges, which make them ideal for cycling.

LOCATION
North Georgia is a mecca for mountain biking and road biking. See p. 135 for a listing of guidebooks detailing the best riding locations.

SEASON
Mountain biking: year-round
Road biking: best April–October

TIME ALLOWANCE
As long as you like.

COST
Free if you have your own bike.
Rentals are available. See p. 138 for a listing of shops with bikes for rent.

BRING ALONG
Bike helmet, water bottle (rental establishments should provide these), shorts and shoes, spare tube, tools, pump, high-energy snack, guidebook or map.

NOTE
You'll need a mountain bike if you plan to ride on trails or gravel roads, but any bicycle with gears will do for the paved roads. A mountain bike will work especially well on pavement if it is equipped with "slicks" (smooth tires). Don't forget your helmet!

Bicycle touring in north Georgia never fails to turn up pleasant surprises along the way.

MOUNTAIN BIKING SEES TREMENDOUS GROWTH

Over the last several years, no group of recreationists has learned better how to become trail volunteers than mountain bikers. In the mid-1980s, few people in north Georgia had even heard of mountain bikes. By the turn of the millennium, mountain bikers had become the number one users of public forest trails in the region. With that kind of user growth, you can bet there were growing pains. The biggest pain of all was trail user conflict. On many of the trails, especially nearer Atlanta, there simply were too many users vying for the same trails.

TRAIL VOLUNTEERS ARE CONSCIENTIOUS CYCLISTS

Conscientious mountain bikers soon realized they had to do something positive or lose the right to ride on the trails, so they became trail volunteers. This meant they worked with the Forest Service and other land agencies to determine what trails needed repair or where new trails needed to be constructed. Then they went out and actually did the work.

VOLUNTEERING IS ESSENTIAL TO RECREATION

These days, volunteers in the forest are essential to maintaining a high level of recreational opportunity. Congress recently has decreased funding for such projects as new trail

Becoming a Mountain Bike Trail Volunteer

construction and maintenance of existing trails on public lands. Without the money for trail building and upkeep, land agencies now depend heavily on groups of bikers, hikers, and horseback riders to do the work. Having trails to use in the future is the pay the volunteers receive for their efforts.

BECOMING A VOLUNTEER IS EASY

You can become a volunteer in several different ways:
1) Call your local forest ranger or a local biking or hiking club and see when the next trail maintenance day is scheduled. Phone numbers for land agencies are listed in the appendix of this book.
2) If you are a cyclist, consider joining the International Mountain Biking Association (303-545-9011 or www.imba.com) or a local affiliated club. IMBA works on a global level to increase cycling opportunities.
3) You might even want to contact your representatives in Washington and let them know you'd like more tax dollars allocated for recreation and trails in the future.

It's important to remember that we have some control over—and some responsibility for—the condition of our forest trails. Volunteering is a great way to contribute.

Camping

National forest campgrounds are found throughout north Georgia.

Camping is one of the most popular natural adventures in America, and there's certainly no shortage of camping opportunities in this region. For an inexpensive and easy camping experience, plan a stay in a national forest or state park campground. These are almost always located in an idyllic setting. If you really want to rough it, head into the backcountry and pick a site of your own.

LOCATION
In national forests, camp anywhere in the backcountry or at designated roadside camp spots. In the national parks, camp at desig-nated backcountry campsites. For public campgrounds in both the national forests and state parks, see the listings on pp. 131–135.

SEASON
April–October or year-round for the hardy

TIME ALLOWANCE
Overnight to one week or more

COST
Free in the backcountry.
$8–15 per site per night in the public campgrounds.

BRING ALONG
All your camping equipment. Be sure to bring large water containers for carrying and storage. Many of the state park and national forest sites do not have hookups.

NOTE
In the national forest, camping spots are taken on a first-come, first-served basis. If you don't want to take any chances with availability, it's possible to book ahead for a state park campsite. Call 800-864-7275 or go to www.gastateparks.org on the Web.

Tents and camping sure have evolved over the years. Baker tent, circa 1920.

FIRES—ONCE A NECESSITY

Since the discovery of fire itself, humans have wanted to keep a fire burning at night while in the wilderness. There were many reasons: a fire could cook a meal, ward off animal predators, and keep a person warm. This fire-burning instinct has carried over into the modern-day camper. Although a fire usually is no longer needed for the above reasons, the fascination with campfire remains.

PICK YOUR SITE AND GATHER YOUR MATERIALS

If you're going to have a fire, do it right. First, you'll need a clear area. Most campgrounds provide a fire ring, but at a primitive site you'll need to clear a space for the fire. Rake away any brush or leaves that could cause the fire to spread, and stay away from low-hanging limbs. Next, gather your firewood. For a quick starting, quiet campfire, look for dry, dead limbs lying on the ground. Break these into smaller, fire-sized pieces that make optimal fuel. Above all, do not cut living trees.

THERE ARE THREE KINDS OF MATERIAL NEEDED TO BUILD A FIRE

To get your fire started, gather a fist-sized bundle of very small dead twigs (the tinder), and an assortment of pieces between twig size (kindling) and your largest pieces (fuel). If the woods are wet from a recent rain, you can almost always

Building the Perfect Campfire

find very small dead twigs still attached to trees that remain dry except in the wettest weather. Arrange your fire material so you can get to everything. Make sure to have enough tinder and kindling so as not to run out before the fire gets going good.

LET YOUR PRIMITIVE SELF ENJOY YOUR CREATION

Now, build your fire. Two methods that work well for building campfires are the lean-to style and the pyramid style. For a lean-to, push a stick into the ground at an angle. Arrange a large amount of tinder under the stick and lean the kindling against the stick all around, leaving room to reach the tinder with a match. The fuel sticks are leaned against the kindling. For a pyramid fire, pretend you are building a log cabin, with the larger sticks at the bottom gradually building up to a point. Stuff the inside with tinder. If you do it correctly, there will be no need for paper. *Never use a dangerous combustible fluid!* Light the fire, sit back, and enjoy.

Horseback Riding

 f you have your own horse, many trails await you in the national forest, the state parks, and even in the military parks. If you don't have a horse but want to give riding a try, there are countless outfitters offering rides of various lengths all across the top of the state. These guided trips can be a lot of fun, especially for children and for those who have never ridden before.

Horseback riding is popular at Chickamauga Battlefield Park.

LOCATION
For horse owners, popular destinations include the **Pinhote Trail** north of Rome, **Chickamauga Battlefield**, **Fort Mountain State Park**, the **Bull Mountain** trails west of Dahlonega, and along the **Chattooga River**. To book guided trips in advance, it's best to ask for a listing of outfitters from the Chamber of Commerce nearest your destination (see appendix, p. 133).

SEASON
Year-round

TIME ALLOWANCE
As long as you like. Guided excursions usually last 1–2 hours.

COST
Outfitters vary, but $9–12 per person per hour is a good rule of thumb.

BRING ALONG
Comfortable riding clothing (loose-fitting long pants are usually best), sturdy shoes or riding boots, camera, sun protection.

NOTE
Many of the trails open to horse use are also open to other users, including mountain bikers and hikers. The rule of thumb is: bikers yield to horses, horses yield to hikers, and hikers yield to no one.

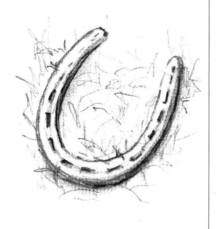

500 YEARS AGO, THERE WERE NO HORSES IN NORTH GEORGIA

Today, horses are a familiar sight in north Georgia. Such was not the case 500 years ago. Native Americans of that time knew nothing of the horse, and all travel was done on foot. Historians have two theories of how the first horses came to north Georgia: they either came north from Florida or east from the western frontier. One thing is for certain—they would have been of Spanish descent.

TRADE WITH FLORIDA TRIBES BROUGHT HORSES TO GEORGIA

Spanish explorers brought horses to Florida as early as 1513. Ponce de Leon and Panfilo de Narvaez led expeditions in the Florida region in 1513, 1521, and 1528. In 1539, Hernando de Soto continued from Florida on into north Georgia and finally to the Mississippi. It is possible that the horses de Soto's men rode were the first seen in north Georgia. Imagine what the Indians must have thought as the explorers came riding into their camp atop beasts they had never seen before.

It's equally possible that by the time de Soto arrived, the horse had preceded him. Trade was well established between the tribes of Georgia and Florida, and horses left behind in America by earlier explorers could easily have made their way north.

North Georgia's First Horses

HORSES ALSO ARRIVED FROM THE WESTERN TERRITORIES

Another theory is that the first horses arrived in north Georgia via trade with Indians from the west. When the Spanish conquered Mexico in 1519 they had a healthy supply of horses with them. These horses are certainly the ancestors of the American western pony, and they also worked their way east on the trading routes. It is known that the Upper Creek tribes who lived in Georgia had horses acquired from the Choctaws, who in turn had acquired them from tribes farther west. Whether they arrived prior to or after those from Florida is not known.

Backpacking

Some views you can only find on foot, like this one on the Appalachian Trail.

An overnight backpacking trip into the mountains is educational, adventuresome, and, most of all, fun. You don't have to go far before the world changes and you're suddenly in a land ruled by the elements. Some beautiful views, waterfalls, plants, and animals can be seen only by those traveling on foot. Although children will usually surprise you with their energy, if you're backpacking with them it's best to keep the distances short and the destinations interesting, ending with a scenic vista or a large meadow. Below are some suggested hiking locations.

LOCATION
- The Cohutta Wilderness
- The Appalachian Trail
- Amicalola Falls State Park (hike-in lodge)
- Fort Mountain State Park
- The Chattooga River Trail

See pp. 128–129 for more details on Appalachian Trail access and backpacking jumping off points, and p. 132 for where to purchase trail maps.

SEASON
Year-round; best in warmer months

TIME ALLOWANCE
As long as you like.

COST
Free

BRING ALONG
Good hiking shoes or boots; comfortable, well-padded, light packs to carry all your gear; camera; water and a means of water purification; guidebooks and maps. A backcountry permit is required in some state parks.

FIRST, LEARN THE ART OF COMPROMISE

Backpacking or hiking with children is a totally different experience than with adults or teenagers. In order for everyone to have a great experience, the adults in the crowd must first learn the art of compromise. Things like walking along very slowly; stopping to look at every other thing; turning around and going back to look at something again even though it's several hundred yards back; or hiking half a mile, camping, and then returning to the trailhead in the morning may not be your idea of the perfect outing. But if you do want to have that "perfect" outing with your kids, you have to be willing to scale it down to meet their needs and interests.

LIMIT YOUR EXPECTATIONS

It only takes one outing to realize that having a lot of expectations is a recipe for disaster. If you think you can cover a lot of miles, climb to the highest peaks, or stay out for nights on end, think again. You may actually be able to do any of these things with your children, but if you automatically expect it, someone—and maybe several someones—is bound to be disappointed. Remember too that every child has her/his own speed and that younger, portable kids usually can go farther than mobile toddlers.

Hiking With Children

HELPFUL HINTS

- Before you head out on that first overnight backpacking trip, take a number of increasingly longer day hikes.
- Children who are unable to walk usually can be transported farther than mobile ones. Just be sure to dress them appropriately—particularly their arms, legs, hands, and feet. Those backpack child carriers can be hot in the summertime and cold in the wintertime.
- Toddlers often will want to walk themselves, and they move very slowly. They also expect to be carried for great distances. If you are backpacking, be prepared to carry your backpack as well as your child and his/her backpack.
- Keep backpacking trips short and make sure the destination has a number of interesting things to see or do along the way.
- If your child is old enough to be carrying a loaded backpack, she/he should be wearing appropriate hiking shoes. Before this age, sneakers do just fine.
- Set a good example by being the model outdoorsperson. Remember—your good habits as well as your bad will be imitated by your children.

Wild Trout Fishing

Fly fishing is popular in small streams as well as large.

here are over 300 streams in the north Georgia mountains representing 5,500 miles of waters designated as Georgia trout streams. That's a lot of streams, and it means one thing for sure— there are a lot of wild trout out there waiting to be caught. Whether you prefer to fish wide open rivers or small hidden creeks, there is no lack of "fishing holes." No matter where you are in the mountains, a trout stream is usually nearby.

FAVORITE LOCATIONS
- **The Cohuttas**
- **Chattahoochee River**
- **Chattooga River**

Call 706-947-3112 and ask for publication "Trout Streams of Georgia," or go to www.ganet.org/dnr for trout fishing information.

SEASON
Streams signed as (YR) are open year-round. Streams marked as (S) are open seasonally, April 1 – October 31.

TIME ALLOWANCE
As long as you like.

COST
Resident License:
One-day: $3.50 + $5.00 trout stamp
Yearly: $9.00 + $5.00 trout stamp
Nonresident License:
One-day: $3.50 + $13.00 trout stamp
Seven-day: $7.00 + $13.00 trout stamp
Season: $24.00 + $13.00 trout stamp

BRING ALONG
Fishing gear, waders, license, picnic, camera.

Casting for Trout

ACCURATE CASTING IS AN ESSENTIAL SKILL FOR CATCHING TROUT

If you've seen the movie or read the book, *A River Runs Through It*, you have come to realize that proper casting of the fly rod is as important to many fly fisherman as actually catching the fish—sometimes more so! Correct casting is seen as an art, a dance, and an act of creativity. It can be achieved only through diligent practice.

GET TO KNOW THE SPORT BEFORE INVESTING IN EQUIPMENT

If you've never fly fished for trout on a stream before, you may want to consider investing in a casting lesson or two. At the least, you'll want to pick up a book or video on the subject. Do this before investing in a rod and equipment. This way, you can decide if fly fishing is for you before relieving your wallet of too much of its contents. Rods alone range in price from $50 to $1,000. Once hooked, you'll want waders, vests, fly-tying equipment, polarized glasses—the works. All this can add up to a pretty expensive hobby. It may help to keep in mind that the fly alone attracts the fish, whether it's attached to the end of a simple stick with a piece of monofilament or the far end of walking fly-fishing shop.

PRACTICE MAKES PERFECT

The essence of the sport, however, is not only catching but outwitting the fish, whose tiny brain you'll swear at times is more ingenious than your own. Learning to cast great distances or to place your fly quietly beneath heavy cover can be quite rewarding. To save frustration out on the stream, it can help to get plenty of practice at home beforehand.

A FLY-CASTING OBSTACLE COURSE CAN HELP

You may even want to set up your own fly-casting obstacle course. Pick an area with plenty of room to zip a fly about, and always remember to remove the hook from your practice flies. Practice casting through tires or hula hoops. Set yourself under a low-hanging tree. Try to place the fly in a tin can from various distances. The sky's the limit. A half hour or so of practice every other day during the week will have you casting like a pro on the weekend for the real thing.

Watersports

Natural adventures in the waters of north Georgia couldn't be more varied. Whitewater activities can be as challenging as rafting on one of America's wild and scenic rivers through a national forest or as laid-back as tubing the cool mountain streams of Alpine Helen. For the very adventurous, there are whitewater kayaking and canoeing opportunities.

North Georgia also boasts a wonderful curiosity you won't find just anywhere—a public swimming pool fed by a natural spring that flows from the entrance of a nearby cave! The pool at Cave Springs is even said to be shaped like the state of Georgia. We'll let you decide.

LAKES OFFER CALMER ALTERNATIVES TO WHITEWATER THRILLS

Many folks don't necessarily associate lakes with north Georgia, which is why we think of them as "hidden." The pleasures to be found there are not to be missed. From Lake Conasauga to Lake Winfield Scott, these well-kept mountain secrets are wonderful places to enjoy not only swimming and boating, but picnicking, hiking, and camping as well.

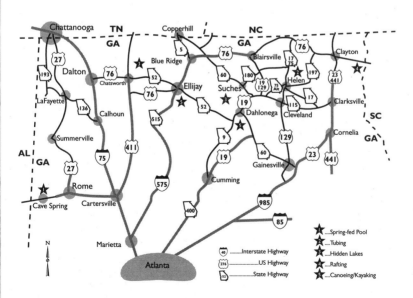

Whitewater Rafting

Challenging the Chattooga's Section IV takes an expert guide.

Rafting is an exciting activity for almost everyone. Outfitters on several rivers in north Georgia provide both rental equipment and guided trips. Most famous of all is the mighty Chattooga River, one of the country's classic runs. You'll crash and splash down a boulder-strewn river and soon find it's the perfect way to cool off on a hot summer day, or to see brilliant spring wildflowers or bright autumn foliage. Many folks make these whitewater adventures the centerpiece of their entire vacation.

LOCATION
- **The Chattooga River**, east of Clayton on the GA-SC border.
- **The Chattahoochee River**, south of Helen.
- **The Chestatee River**, near Dahlonega.

See p. 138 for a list of outfitters.

SEASON
April–October

TIME ALLOWANCE
Half day to full day

COST
Rentals: $13–22 per person.
Guided trips: $64–99 per person.
Prices vary between individual outfitters; different rivers; and for age, group size, and time of year.

BRING ALONG
Change of clothes, towel, T-shirt, bathing suit or swim trunks, old shoes you don't mind getting wet, waterproof camera, and snacks or a picnic for after the trip.

NOTE
The minimum age for the Chattooga is 10 for Section III and 13 for Section IV.

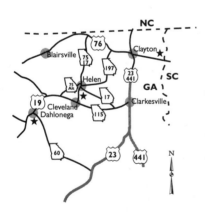

Restrooms
Picnic Tables
Handicapped Access

YOU MAY HAVE A GUIDE IN YOUR RAFT—OR NOT

Depending on the river or the section of river, when you go whitewater rafting you'll either be assigned a guide or issued a raft and expected to go it on your own. Any reputable rafting company will provide some instruction before turning you loose. So you'll have an idea of what you're getting into before you get there, here's what you'll need to know to guide your own raft.

EVERY BOAT NEEDS A CAPTAIN

Every boat needs a captain, so you'll select one for yours. Once a captain is chosen, he or she is given control of the boat. The captain's job is to steer the raft where it needs to go to make it safely down the river, but that job can't be done alone— the crew must work as a team. Successful captains bring out the best in their crews and don't try to muscle the raft around all by themselves. Good communication skills are just as important as technical skills.

THE CAPTAIN STEERS, WHILE THE CREW IS THE MOTOR

The captain takes a position in the back of the raft, as near to center as possible and where she/he can see the river ahead. The remainder of

How to Guide Your Own Raft

the crew is placed equally along either side. Feet are kept inside the craft, preferably braced under the inflated tube, or thwart. For the most part, the crew acts as the motor of the craft, while the captain uses his/her paddle like a rudder to adjust the angle of the boat.

Turning the raft is accomplished by the crew on one side backpaddling while the crew on the other side paddles forward. The boat maneuvers best when moving faster or slower than the river current. For the smoothest run, crew members should do only as the captain asks. Attempting to steer the boat from the front or sides only leads to confusion.

PRACTICE MAKES PERFECT

The first thing to do when you get on the river is practice. The captain can call commands for "all forward" or "all back" while she or he practices steering. Make sure to also try the more complicated commands like "left side back, right side forward," which will spin the boat. Crew members must be able to hear the captain above the roar of the rapids. And the captain must remember to tell the crew when to stop paddling or to take a break.

You'll encounter many situations calling for ingenuity as you descend the river. Mastering these basic skills will help you enjoy the river while running it with some control.

Tubing

On a hot day, tubing a cool creek can't be beat.

 n a hot summer day, this is one of the best adventures going! You're sure to cool off as you float lazily down the river, bumping into rocks and spinning like a pinball through the shallow rapids. Hook arms and feet with your friends and form a tube train to snake your way down, or see who can go the farthest without getting stuck. However you do it, you can be certain of two things: you're going to get wet and you're going to have fun!

LOCATION
The most popular tubing destination in north Georgia is the Chattahoochee River in Helen. See p. 138 for a list of tubing outfitters.

SEASON
June–August

TIME ALLOWANCE
As long as you like, but most folks are ready for a break after 3–4 hours.

COST
Tubes rent for around $5–8 per day. If you have your own tube, use of the river is free.

BRING ALONG
Change of clothes, towel, T-shirt, swim trunks, old shoes you don't mind getting wet, waterproof camera, picnic, sun protection.

NOTE
For those with their own tubes, a number of roadside streams in north Georgia are suitable for tubing, and the only expense is getting there. Most tire repair centers will be glad to sell you an old innertube, and you can fashion a seat for it yourself.

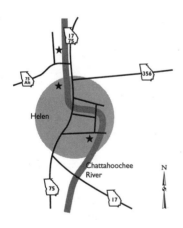

Helen

Chattahoochee River

N

Restrooms
Picnic Tables

CHOOSING YOUR TUBE

There are many tube rental establishments in the mountains, and the price of a single tube for a day is quite reasonable. When perusing those rings of rubber, you'll see that there are two basic types—those with seats and those without. Usually, those without are a little less expensive to rent, but if you're given a choice, get a tube with a seat!

Here's why: seatless tubes are best for deep, slow moving rivers or lakes, but the seated variety are a must on rocky mountain streams. That small wooden board serves two purposes: First, it gives you a little more space to edge up out of the water. More importantly, it protects your behind from taking some pretty good bumps and bruises on the rocks.

WEAR THE RIGHT FOOTGEAR

In most areas, floating down the creek is the easy part. Going back to float a rapid again requires walking. And walking in soggy clothes and wet shoes while carrying a bulky tube over sometimes rocky, rooty terrain can be a challenge. Make sure to wear sturdy footgear that you don't mind getting wet. Going barefoot is a bad idea.

THE WATER CAN BE COLD!

As for clothing, remember that mountain streams can be chilly, and

Tips for Tubing

at least some of the time you'll be in the shade. On hot days many folks are fine in just a bathing suit. Wearing a light synthetic T-shirt can feel pretty good and will also offer some sun protection. If you get cold very easily, consider wearing a light nylon jacket—something you can tie around your waist or the tube seat if you find you don't need it.

TUBING TECHNIQUE

Tubing itself is quite easy. Sit in the center of the tube, trying your best to keep your feet pointing downstream so you can use them to push off the rocks. Use your hands as paddles to adjust your direction. Then just let the current pull you along. Stuck on a rock? Try bouncing up and down and pushing off the rock to one side or the other. If this doesn't work, step down in the water and shove off. Step carefully, because the creek bed can be pretty slippery.

Hidden Lakes

There is nothing more peaceful than a canoe trip on a quiet lake.

Scattered throughout the mountains of north Georgia are a number of small, hidden lakes that are serene, beautiful, and make for great places to enjoy quiet water recreation. These are not to be confused with the large, noisy reservoirs with their power boats and hundreds of miles of shoreline. For most of these lakes you can see the entire body of water from one spot and walk all the way around it in a short time. You might enjoy fishing, canoeing, swimming, or just relaxing along the water's edge. Artist types might even want to bring along their easels.

THE LAKES

Lake Conasauga
Highest lake in Georgia. 19 acres. Camping, picnicking, hiking, swimming, boating, and fishing. See map, p. 139.

Lake Winfield Scott
High mountain, 18-acre lake with camping, picnicking, swimming, boating, hiking, and fishing. On GA 180, five miles east of Suches. See map, p. 139.

Dockery Lake
Popular three-acre trout lake with camping, picnicking, and hiking. On Forest Route 654 off GA 60 south of Suches.

Rock Creek Lake
Most hidden lake of all. Fishing and boating. Picnicking and camping nearby. See map, p. 139.

LOCATION
Suggested locations at left

SEASON
Year-round

TIME ALLOWANCE
Anything from a brief stop to a weekend camp-out by the lake.

COST
Most are free, although there may be a small daily use fee for some in the national forest.

BRING ALONG
Camera, picnic, swim trunks, sun protection, canoe, fishing rod and license, hiking shoes.

NOTE
Just getting to some of these lakes is half the adventure. Other than Lake Winfield Scott, the lakes are located on forest dirt roads. You may want to combine a visit to one of these with an off-pavement driving excursion.

How to Tell a Lake From a Pond

USING THE CORRECT TERM IS COMPLICATED

Sometimes the simplest questions have the most complicated answers. This seems to be the case when it comes to the difference between lakes and ponds. Obviously, you'd never refer to Lake Erie as a pond, nor would you refer to a mud puddle as a lake. But as the bodies of water get closer and closer in size, correct terminology for them becomes less and less clear.

WEBSTER'S SAYS A POND IS SMALLER THAN A LAKE

According to *Webster's Dictionary*, a lake is "an inland body of usually fresh water, larger than a pool or pond, generally formed by some obstruction in the course of flowing water." Sounds simple enough. Also according to *Webster's*, a pond is "a body of water smaller than a lake, often artificially formed." Now it's getting complicated! Looks like the folks at *Webster's* don't have it figured out either.

IN GREEK, LAKE MEANS POND!

Okay, let's check the encyclopedia. In the *World Book*, there's a much more detailed definition. "A lake is a body of water surrounded by land. Lakes may be found in all parts of the world. Some large bodies of water commonly known as seas are really lakes. The word "lake" comes from the Greek word *lakkos*, meaning *hole* or *pond*." Pond! Confused yet?

AND THE ANSWER IS ...

So what does the *World Book* have to say about ponds? "A pond is a small, quiet body of water that is usually shallow enough for sunlight to reach the bottom. The sunlight enables rooted plants to grow across a pond bottom from shore to shore." This is the most convincing definition yet. But on closer examination you'll see it's not absolutely definitive. Notice the phrase "usually shallow enough." Evidently there are ponds that are not shallow enough for sunlight to reach the bottom. And what do you call Lake Mattamuskeet in North Carolina or Mille Lacs Lake in Minnesota, both so big you can't see the other side, but with an average depth of three feet?

We'll leave the question for you to ponder and decide.

Canoeing & Kayaking

Not all of North Georgia's rivers are rollicking whitewater.

For those who have their own boats, there are many options for kayaking and canoeing all across north Georgia. You'll find everything from serious, demanding whitewater to quiet, gentle streams. Along some rivers, outfitters offer rentals and instruction for first-timers wanting to give river boating a try. Seeing the wilderness from a boat can be one of the most enjoyable things you'll ever do. It's no wonder some enthusiasts spend almost every weekend exploring north Georgia's rivers or streams.

LOCATION
The **Chattooga, Chattahoochee, Cartecay,** and **Chestatee** are the most popular rivers. Check the appendix on p. 135 for a list of river guidebooks and on p. 138 for a list of outfitters offering rentals.

SEASON
April–October (year-round for the hardy!)

TIME ALLOWANCE
Half day to all day

COST
Free if you own your own gear; $20–40 for rentals.

BRING ALONG
Change of clothes, towel, T-shirt, swim trunks, old shoes you don't mind getting wet, waterproof camera, high-energy snacks, sun protection, proper lifejackets and paddling gear.

NOTE
Want to try whitewater boating on your own but don't think you're up for a canoe or kayak? Ask an outfitter about inflatable kayaks. They're loads of fun and easy to use.

Inflatable kayaks take much less time to learn how to maneuver than a canoe or regular kayak.

A SAFE RIVER TRIP IS A GOOD RIVER TRIP

Regardless of whether you are paddling a boat on a quietwater river or a thundering whitewater monster, following river safety rules is essential. Quietwater is a bit easier and requires fewer skills than whitewater does, but whichever you choose, here are some techniques you will want to learn.

QUIETWATER SAFETY

- Know your craft and its limitations.
- Always wear a Coast Guard-approved personal flotation device (PFD) or life vest.
- Never boat alone in unfamiliar waters without letting someone know your trip plan.
- If you are not familiar with the river, study a map or guidebook ahead of time, and then carry it with you.
- Carry extra equipment, as well as a first-aid kit. Know the kit's contents and how to use them.
- Leave the booze at home. Never paddle while under the influence of alcohol or drugs.

WHITEWATER SAFETY

- Follow the rules for quietwater safety above with this exception: never boat alone.
- Carry a throw rope in each boat.
- At least one (preferably everyone) in the party should have completed a river safety course and know the use of ropes, carabiners, prussiks, etc., for rescue techniques.

River Safety

- Keep to rivers that are within your ability level. Challenge yourself on these before advancing to more difficult rivers.
- In the event of a swim, keep your feet up and pointed downstream while in the rapids.
- Set fellow paddlers in strategic spots for safety in major rapids. They may be in boats or on shore with ropes, or both.
- Know exit points along the river in case evacuation becomes necessary.

SUGGESTED READING

River Rescue by Bechdel and Ray (AMC Books, 1997)

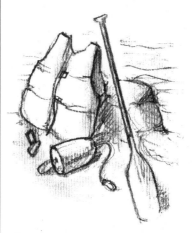

Proper gear is an important part of a safe river trip.

Cave Spring Pool

The shade by the pool is almost as refreshing as the pool itself.

You might not think a swimming pool fits into the category of a natural adventure until you arrive at the Cave Spring Pool. This is not your typical swimming pool. It's huge (over an acre and a half) and is constructed of stone and mortar. Don't expect a white painted bottom with lines either, although the water is crystal clear. It is fed by the chilly, 56° waters of the Cave Spring. This water is cold! It is also *very* refreshing on a hot northwest Georgia day.

LOCATION
Rolater Park in the heart of Cave Spring. 706-777-8439.

SEASON
Memorial Day to Labor Day
Open Wednesday–Saturday, 10 am – 6 pm;
Sunday, 1–6 pm.
Closed Monday–Tuesday for cleaning.

TIME ALLOWANCE
From a short cooling dip to all day if you like.

COST
Adults: $3
Children 6 and under: $1
Seniors 62+: free

BRING ALONG
Change of clothes, towel, swimsuit, sun protection, snacks or a picnic, something to float on.

NOTE
Adjacent to the pool is the Cave Spring Cave (p. 86). You may want to take in both—along with a picnic—for a great day's outing. Bring an empty jug to fill with water from the spring and take some of that cool, natural H_2O home with you.

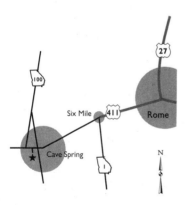

Restrooms
Picnic Tables
Handicapped Access

Mountain Springs

THERE ARE THOUSANDS OF SPRINGS IN THE NORTH GEORGIA MOUNTAINS

If you follow a small stream or rivulet far enough back up in the mountains, you're sure at some point to find a spring. Some of these springs gush out of the side of the mountain with such force as to instantly start a sizable stream. Others seep out so quietly that they only appear as damp spots on the ground. In the mountains of north Georgia there are thousands of springs. In fact, it is from these very springs that mighty Georgia rivers such as the Chattahoochee, the Coosa, and the Savannah are first born.

SPRINGS ARE GREAT PLACES TO TAKE A BREAK

Water from a mountain spring is pure, clear, and cold as it bubbles up from the depths of the earth. Often the spring will include a small, sandy

pool outlined with watercress, a mountain delicacy and a tangy addition to a salad. At the source, the water may be drunk with little concern about contamination. Along the Appalachian Trail, springs are found by following blue-blazed side trails marking their location. While driving, you may notice along the roadways an occasional small pipe sticking out of the side of the mountain with water running out. This is a spring whose access has been made a little easier. Sometimes a tin cup will be hanging next to the pipe, the better to catch the water and sample it. These spots are great places to take a break and have a drink.

GROUNDWATER IS THE SOURCE OF A SPRING

Springs are formed where, for various reasons, ground water makes its way to the surface. It could be gravity forcing the water to rise until it finds a way out to the surface, or a deep crack or fault at the foot of a slope that allows the water to seep or bubble out. If you could dig a great slice from deep out of the earth, you would see many pockets of water—some small, some veritable rivers. When one of these channels meets the earth's surface, a spring is formed.

Auto Touring

North Georgia is blessed with a number of designated scenic byways but, more importantly, with many interesting stops along the way. Some are the handiwork of Mother Nature, and some have been enhanced, organized, and highlighted by human beings.

In your wanderings, you're sure to find a classic country store or two, as they are well preserved in these mountains. Historic courthouses dot the landscape. One now houses the Dahlonega Gold Museum; a few date back to Civil War days and have their own fascinating history. For a lesson in how riverboats once ruled the waterways, visit the Lock & Dam Park in Rome. And don't miss the lovely, vast campus of Berry College, home of one of the world's tallest waterwheels.

MOUNTAIN ROADS OFFER A VARIETY OF THINGS TO SEE

The William Weinman Mineral Museum offers a treasure trove of information on gems found in north Georgia; you'll also learn about its fossils here. Finally, no auto tour is complete without a stop at the apple orchards, where you can sample and buy apples fresh off the tree by the bag, peck, or bushel.

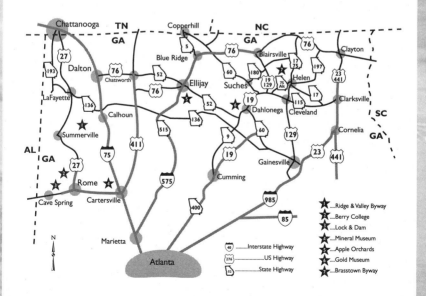

Ridge & Valley Scenic Byway

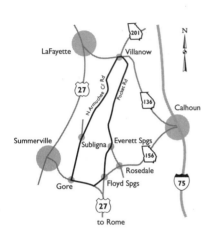

This is a 47-mile loop in what is termed the "ridge and valley" section of northwest Georgia. The ridges you see on either side of you as you drive along are those of Johns Mountain, Taylors Ridge, Little Sand Mountain, and Horn Mountain. You'll travel through The Pocket and alongside Johns Creek and Armuchee (pronounced Ar-MUR-chee) Creek. Much of the route is through rural farmland, with ridges rising up from the valley floor.

LOCATION
The route lies between Dalton and Rome and follows US 27, GA 136, and the North Armuchee Creek, Gore-Subligna, Everett Springs, and Pocket Roads. A good starting point is the Villanow Country Store at the intersection of GA 136 and GA 201.

SEASON
Year-round

TIME ALLOWANCE
2–5 hours, depending on how often you stop.

COST
Free

BRING ALONG
Camera, binoculars, picnic, walking shoes.

NOTE
This route passes country stores in Villanow and in Subligna (p. 63). It also passes through The Pocket Recreation Area (p. 134), near the Johns Mountain Overlook, and by Keown Falls (p. 91). This area is rich with fossils.

This old barn is in "The Pocket."

300 MILLION YEARS IS A LONG TIME

As you drive along this scenic byway, it's hard to imagine that the valleys and ridges you're traversing were once the bottom of a vast sea floor. Of course, it has been well over 300 million years since then, and a lot can change in that amount of time. Still, all indications are that the sea once covered the area.

FOSSILS HAVE BEEN LEFT BEHIND

Some of the most telltale signs of this ancient sea are the fossils it left behind. Road cuts have exposed remains like *crinoid* stems, from an ancient plant resembling a lily, and *brachiopods,* which resemble modern-day clams. One of the best places to look for these is along the Forest Service roads on Taylors Ridge. It takes a keen eye, and it helps to have an idea of what these

Break open a rock and look closely; it may reveal ancient fossils.

Imagine a Vast Sea Here, Millions of Years Ago

fossils look like, but once you get the idea, they are fun to collect. Other places to look for fossils are in the exposed rock faces where highways and secondary roads have been cut through a mountainside.

THE VERY ROCKS WERE FORMED FROM THE SEA

Students of geology will recognize that the ridges themselves are made up of sandstone, chert, and siltstone—all derived from this ancient sea. Sandstone is formed from compressed sea sand, siltstone from the silt, and chert, a component of limestone, from the dead plant matter in the sea.

FISH EYES

One of the best places to get an overview of the entire ridge and valley section of Georgia is from the Johns Mountain Overlook atop Johns Mountain along the byway. From this prominent point, take a look out over the area and imagine what it must have looked like 300 million years ago. For one, John's Mountain itself would be under water. But if you *could* have found a vantage point to view it all, what a sight it would have been! Quite different from today's pastoral scenes of barns, hayfields, and grazing cattle.

Russell/Brasstown Scenic Byway

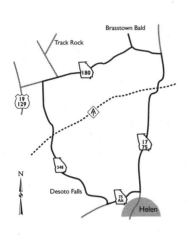

On this 38-mile loop you'll experience Georgia's highest mountains. Starting in Helen, the route bisects two wilderness areas (Raven Cliffs Wilderness and Mark Trail Wilderness) as it climbs to Hogpen Gap. Here you'll cross the Appalachian Trail and put it in low gear for the descent down the other side. After crossing the valley you'll climb up through Jacks Gap and all the way to the top of Brasstown Bald—at 4,784 feet, Georgia's highest peak. The last gap you'll conquer is Unicoi Gap, where you'll cross the Appalachian Trail again. The descent back to Helen is along the headwaters of the Chattahoochee River.

LOCATION
The route begins in Helen and follows GA· 17/75, GA Alt. 75, GA 348, and GA 180.

SEASON
Year-round unless closed by snow

TIME ALLOWANCE
2–4 hours

COST
Free

BRING ALONG
Camera, binoculars, picnic, a full tank of gas.

NOTE
Off GA 180, stop at Track Rock (p. 106). The Chattahoochee River is popular for tubing (p. 46). Drive off-pavement down through the Chattahoochee watershed from Unicoi Gap along Forest Service Route 44 or past High Shoals Falls and through Indian Grave Gap on Forest Service Routes 283 and 79 (p. 139).

A view of the Brasstown Bald Wilderness from Brasstown Bald.

UNDISTURBED VIEWS

As you travel the Russell/Brasstown Scenic Byway, you'll view large tracts of uninhabited mountain land which have no roads or houses. There's a good reason for that: much of it is designated wilderness. To the west of GA 348 is the Raven Cliffs Wilderness Area. Between GA 17/75 and GA 348 is the Mark Trail Wilderness Area, and along the flanks of Brasstown Bald is the Brasstown Bald Wilderness Area. What are these wilderness areas, and how and why were they created?

THE WILDERNESS ACT

In the late 1950s and early 1960s, conservationists worked nationwide to have the Wilderness Act passed in order to formally create a National Wilderness Preservation System. Proponents felt that wilderness offers people solitude, inspiration, natural quiet, and a place to get away. At the same time,

A True Wilderness

designated wilderness protects the biodiversity on which human existence depends. The Wilderness Act of 1964 directed the Forest Service, National Park Service, and the Fish and Wildlife Service to survey their roadless lands for possible wilderness designation. The act requires that wilderness areas be "administered for the use and enjoyment of the American people in such a manner as will leave them unimpaired for future use and enjoyment as wilderness."

NO ROADS, DAMS, OR PERMANENT STRUCTURES

The Wilderness Act protects Congressionally-designated wilderness areas from roads, dams, or other permanent structures. It also protects such lands from timber-cutting, the operation of motorized vehicles and equipment, from bicycle use, and, in many places, horse use. Since 1984 it has prohibited new mining claims and mineral leasing in wilderness areas.

KEEPING IT AS WILD AND NATURAL AS POSSIBLE

You won't see anyone using chain saws or power equipment in the wilderness; only hand tools are allowed. You won't see many trail signs or blazes either. The overall goal for managing these lands is to help them stay as wild and natural as possible. Keep this in mind as you gaze out over the wilderness lands adjacent to the byway.

Off-Pavement Exploring

Many of these roads are suitable for most cars.

Clear days bring great views.

North Georgia's mountains are laced with dirt roads ideal for exploring in sport utility vehicles. You won't always need an SUV, though. Many are negotiable in just about any vehicle that has good tires and ground clearance. The Chattahoochee National Forest maintains a network of roads that traverse some of Georgia's highest ridges. Not to be confused with designated off-road vehicle (ORV) or all-terrain vehicle (ATV) areas, these roads are marked with brown signs and given Forest Service (FS) road status. They'll take you to waterfalls, hikes, through stands of beautiful hardwood forests, to remote primitive camping areas, and to some of the loveliest vistas in Georgia.

LOCATION
Throughout the mountains of north Georgia. See pp. 138–139 for a list of suggested routes.

SEASON
Year-round, although you'll want to avoid these roads during periods of heavy snowfall or during very wet weather.

TIME ALLOWANCE
A few hours to a weekend motoring campout.

COST
Free

BRING ALONG
Camera, binoculars, picnic, hiking shoes, drinking water, camping equipment, good map.

NOTE
Standard Georgia traffic laws apply to these roads, although they rarely have signs.

DRIVING ON DIRT IS A DIFFERENT EXPERIENCE

Driving a vehicle on a winding, rocky, steep mountain road is a good bit different than traveling on smooth asphalt. Even if you're accustomed to it, it's a good idea to take things slow and be extra careful. Here are some driving tips to help ensure a safe and enjoyable experience.

SLOW DOWN!

First of all, slow down—*really* slow down. A vehicle does not respond the same way on loose stones and dirt as it does on a paved surface. Too much speed, and you'll drift dangerously to the outside of curves, where safe braking becomes an impossibility. Remember—the idea of driving these roads is to enjoy the scenery, not to make time.

KEEP BOTH EYES ON THE ROAD

While driving, keep both eyes on the road. If you want to take a look at a view, stop the car right there in the middle of the road if you need

Driving Tips

to (as long as you're not on a blind curve!) and then take a look. Chances are, no one is behind you, and you can move on or pull over if someone comes along.

WATCH THOSE STUTTER BUMPS

Without constant grading, even the slightest uphill will eventually develop ripply, corrugated bumps. You're most likely to run into them on the inside of uphill curves, but they can crop up almost anywhere. Hit these with any speed at all and they can bounce you right off the road—not to mention rattling your car as well as your teeth.

BLIND CURVES CAN BE DANGEROUS

Approach blind curves with caution. Some roads are single-lane with turnouts designed for passing. On a curve, keep to your side of the road and take it slow. You could meet an oncoming vehicle—and it may be a big logging truck, taking up the entire road.

KEEP AN EYE TO THE WEATHER

Avoid these roads altogether during inclement weather. Winter snows can turn a mountain road into a toboggan course, and heavy rains or freezing and then thawing temperatures can turn the hard-packed roadbed into mush. Lastly, always fill up your gas tank before heading out.

North Georgia's Country Stores

With our cities, chain convenience stores, and strip malls spreading farther and farther into rural areas, old time country stores are becoming scarce. In north Georgia, though, the country store is alive and well. These relics from the past are a pleasant surprise to find and explore on a driving outing. They're usually pretty easy to spot—peeling paint on clapboard siding, an old gas pump or two out front, some rockers or an old church pew on the porch. The door is probably propped open, and if you venture inside you'll see a vast array of merchandise—everything from pickled eggs, to nuts and bolts, to fishing supplies, laundry soap, and ice cream sandwiches. Along the walls will be deer antlers and stuffed fish. You may see old farming tools hanging from the ceiling. Best of all, there is usually a warm hello from behind the counter and always something cool to drink.

LOCATION
Scattered along the backroads of north Georgia's counties. See the next page for a selected list of stores and their locations.

SEASON
Year-round

TIME ALLOWANCE
You can spend anywhere from a few minutes to an hour or so exploring the store or sitting in the shade outside, enjoying those pickled eggs and chatting with the owner.

COST
Free to enter, but it is polite to buy something.

BRING ALONG
Camera, spare change.

You can find just about anything at the Villanow Country Store.

VILLANOW COUNTRY STORE

Located east of LaFayette in northwest Georgia at the junction of GA 136 and GA 201, the old store at Villanow is a classic. Outside are working but antiquated gas pumps and shady places to sit alongside more modern drink machines. Inside you'll find wood floors, hunting and fishing trophies mounted on the wall, and farm implements hanging from the ceiling. The store is small, but along the aisles you'll find just about every-thing imaginable.

SUBLIGNA STORE

This old store is just south of the Villanow store at the junction of Armuchee Creek Road and the Gore-Subligna Road, on the Ridge and Valley Scenic Byway (p. 56) route. There is a nice old church pew outside in the shade. Inside you'll find all the necessities you'll ever need—and more.

TALKING ROCK GENERAL STORE

Located in the little village of Talking Rock on GA 136 just east of the GA 5/515 throughway, this quaint little store has all the appearances of an old country store from the outside. Although it now sells more antiques and memorabilia than everyday necessaries, it's still a great stop.

Stores You Don't Want to Miss

CROSSROADS GROCERY

To reach this store, travel east on GA 52 about 10 miles from Ellijay. At present it's a Phillips 66 station as well as a store, and believe it or not, they still pump your gas! Inside you'll find all the classic country store amenities.

OLD SAUTEE STORE

Just south of Helen at the junction of GA 17 and GA 255, the Old Sautee Store is near enough to the tourist town of Helen to absorb some of the Helen tourist tradition. Outside it looks old and rugged; inside you'll find it caters to the tourist trade, selling everything from T-shirts to Christmas ornaments. Crowds in the store can be quite large during peak season. Still, it once *was* a real country store, and if you're in the area, it's worth a visit.

They still pump your gas at Crossroads Grocery near Ellijay.

Lock & Dam Park

Fishing or just sitting and watching other people fish are popular pastimes at the Lock & Dam Park.

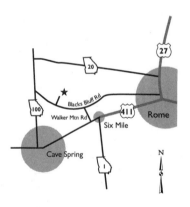

Store
Camping
Restrooms
Picnic Tables
Handicapped Access

Situated on the Coosa River between Rome and the Alabama line are a lock and dam built in 1913 and maintained until 1931 to facilitate riverboat traffic to Rome. Their remains now stand as a reminder of days gone by, when goods were transported not by truck but by great boats on the river. Now the area is a favorite fishing, hiking, and camping destination. The trading post on the park grounds has an exhibit room depicting the old riverboat days, as well as local flora and fauna and early Native American life in the area.

LOCATION
On the Coosa River west of Rome. Take US 27 south to Walker Mountain Road or GA 20 west to GA 100 to Blacks Bluff Road.
706-234-5001
www.romegeorgia.com/sgseeing.html

SEASON
Year-round

TIME ALLOWANCE
1–2 hours to see the lock and dam and exhibit area, to all day if you hike, boat, or fish.

COST
$2 parking fee.
Camping fee is $15–18.

BRING ALONG
Camera, binoculars, picnic, walking shoes, canoe or boat, fishing rod.

NOTE
In spring, when the crappie and striped bass in Lake Weiss make an annual run up the river, the parking lot is packed with fishermen. There's hardly a free space to stand atop the lock, and the tailwaters below the dam are chock full of boats. It's quite a spectacle to see and even more fun to be a part of.

THE AGE OF RIVERBOATS

In the middle of the 19th century, riverboating was a thriving trade in the United States. Paddlewheel steamers plied our nation's rivers, carrying goods from town to town. In north Georgia few of the rivers were navigable except by very small craft. The exception was the mighty Coosa River and its tributaries. In Rome, the Etowah and Oostanaula come together to form the Coosa, and boats traveled from here down into Alabama to Gadsden, Montgomery, and, finally, to Mobile and the Gulf. It's easy to imagine how, in that era, the port of Rome was a hubbub of activity. North Georgia cotton was being shipped south while people traveled to and fro.

WHAT'S IN A NAME?

Then as now, the name of a boat suggested the limits of its owner's imagination. Many of the boats that served Rome took their names from the rivers themselves. There were the *Coosa*, the *Connasauga*, and the *Etowah Bill*. Others were named for nearby towns—the *Calhoun*, the *Alfareta*, the *Hill City* (Rome). Surely the *Economic* must have been owned by someone seeking a fortune, while the *Magnolia*'s owner must have pursued more botanical or aesthetic interests. The least imaginative just named the boats after themselves—the *John J. Seay*, the *Willie Wagnon*, the *John Warlock*.

Riverboats of the Past

And what fleet in the South would be complete without a *Dixie*?

MAYO'S LOCK AND DAM

Until 1913, any boat traveling to or from Rome had to negotiate the treacherous waters of Mayo's Bar. In that year the final lock and dam of a series between Rome and Gadsden were completed—the ones at Rome's Lock and Dam Park. The improved navigability must have seemed a godsend for riverboat pilots.

Unfortunately, only two or three boats took advantage of the improved situation. By then railroads had all but taken over the transportation business. In 1931 maintenance of Mayo's Lock and Dam by the US Army Corps of Engineers was halted.

Paddlewheel steamers regularly plied the Coosa River.

Berry College

Berry College boasts one of the largest overshot waterwheels in the world.

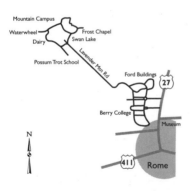

Restrooms
Picnic Tables
Handicapped Access
Gift Shop

ou might not think a college campus makes much of a driving tour, much less a natural adventure. If this is the case, you've never been to Berry College. Situated at the foot of Lavender Mountain in northwest Georgia, Berry has one of the largest campuses in the world—over 28,000 acres. As you tour it, you'll find historic log cabins, castle-like stone buildings, a variety of cattle (including Longhorns), a museum, an historic antebellum home, one of the highest waterwheels in the world, a classic European-style dairy, and probably more deer than you'll see anywhere else in Georgia.

LOCATION
Just north of Rome on US 27.
706-232-5374
www.berry.edu

SEASON
The campus is open year-round.
Classes are in session most months.

TIME ALLOWANCE
Half day to all day

COST
Free.
Admission charge to Martha Berry House & Museum (adults: $5; children 6–12: $3)

BRING ALONG
Camera, binoculars, picnic, walking shoes.

NOTE
You'll enter the campus through a gate with a guardhouse. Most days, you just roll right through the open gate. Ask the guard for a self-guided tour map. Unless there is a special occasion, the campus is closed to visitors at night.

Martha Berry's Dream

A WOMAN BORN INTO WEALTH AND PRIVILEGE

Martha Berry was born into a wealthy home where nearly any need or desire she ever had was met. Such was not the case for most children growing up in the north Georgia mountains following the Civil War. Folks were poor, with little money for food, let alone schooling. In 1900, at a tiny mountain church (now called Possum Trot) not too far from her home, Martha Berry began teaching Sunday school classes for these mountain children. It was during this time she decided they needed an education and she would provide it.

EDUCATING MOUNTAIN CHILDREN

In January of 1902, Miss Berry founded the Boy's Industrial School. Boys from across the nearby mountains were encouraged to attend. They would not have to pay, but they were expected to work— and work they did. Over the years as the school grew, buildings were built and the land was farmed. In 1908, the Martha Berry School for Girls opened, and by 1922 the school not only offered primary and secondary grades, but had become an accredited college as well—Berry College as it is known today.

WORK-STUDY PROGRAM REMAINS AT THE COLLEGE

Through the years, students have always worked for their education— and the policy is still loosely in effect today. Many of the buildings you see as you tour the campus, as well as the roads you drive on, were built by student hands. And not only did they raise the buildings, they first made the bricks and milled the timber! This inspired woman and her innovative ideas attracted the concerns and dollars of a number of very influential people. Some of the most notable were Henry Ford, Charles Dana, and Andrew Carnegie, who gave huge sums to help Martha Berry ensure that her dream would be complete. You'll find their names attached to the buildings they helped make a reality. Martha Berry died in 1942, but her vision to educate the children of north Georgia lives on.

Henry Ford helped Miss Berry with her dream by financing these Gothic-style stone buildings.

William Weinman Mineral Museum

Children love to dig for fossils at the mineral museum.

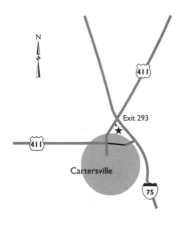

Restrooms
Picnic Tables
Handicapped Access
Gift Shop

Located within sight of I-75 near Cartersville, this mineral museum is a real gem. Outside is an exhibit of historical mining equipment, including a Whitcomb Locomotive from 1930. Inside, the Georgia room has a dark cave—much like the many caves scattered about northwest Georgia—and cases highlighting the different geological regions of the state. Children love the discovery room, where you can search for fossilized dinosaur and other skeletons. Other rooms display minerals and fossils from around the world, and there is an extensive regional geology library.

LOCATION
From I-75, take Exit 293 onto US 411. The museum is located on the southwest side of the interstate behind motels and gas stations.
770-386-0576
http://morgan.chara.gsu.edu/~weinman/

SEASON
Year-round. Tuesday–Saturday, 10:00 am – 4:30 pm; Sunday, 2:00–4:30 pm.
Closed on Mondays and holidays.

TIME ALLOWANCE
1–2 hours

COST
Adults: $3.50
Children: $2.50 (under 6, free)
Seniors: $2.00

BRING ALONG
Picnic, camera, questions.

NOTE
The Etowah Indian Mounds are nearby (p. 94). The two together make a great day's outing.

The Georgia Carpet Industry

AN INDUSTRY IS BORN

You don't have to travel up and down I-75 (or any other road) between Atlanta and Chattanooga more than once to realize that carpet is a big deal in north Georgia. In fact, the town of Dalton claims the distinction of "the carpet capital of the world." Nowadays, most every community in the corridor between Cartersville and Dalton has one, two, or an abundance of carpet manufacturing plants. Why north Georgia? This certainly isn't Turkey, where nomadic tribes once carried their houses around with them and then laid out ornate carpets to use for their floors.

IT STARTED AS A HOME BUSINESS

In the early part of the 1900s, the economy of northwest Georgia was not so flush. Most folks were downright poor. To earn extra money, a woman named Catherine Evans Whitener began using an American tufting technique known as "candle-wick embroidery" to make bedspreads to sell. She made a lot of them. Her bedspreads were liked so well she soon formed the Evans Manufacturing Company and taught other women the skill of hand-tufting.

ROUTE 41 BECOMES "BEDSPREAD ALLEY"

Route 41 was then the major route between Atlanta and Chattanooga. In the 1920s, all along the way the traveler would see tufted chenille and drape bedspreads hanging from the front porches of homes. In those days the road became known as "Chenille" or "Bedspread Alley." Some people even called it "Peacock Alley" for the most famous bedspread design. Businessmen traveling back and forth would buy the bedspreads to take home as gifts for their wives.

BEDSPREADS TRANSFORM INTO WALL-TO-WALL CARPET

One thing led to another, and eventually the bedspread industry evolved into the tufted carpet industry—the predominant way of making carpets today. The popularity of wall-to-wall carpeting exploded into American homes, and today Dalton is unrivaled in its production of carpet. Almost 90% of the functional carpet produced worldwide is made within a 25-mile radius of the town.

WHAT'S ALL THIS TO DO WITH A MINERAL MUSEUM?

Many of the dyes used to color carpets today contain barite. This mineral is found in north Georgia and is mined near the mineral museum in Cartersville.

Historic Courthouses

Some courthouses, like the one in Murray County, sit atop a rise in the town square.

Bartow County's courthouse is in its third location in Cartersville.

Travel along the backroads of north Georgia is bound to take you into one of the many county seats. And right in the middle of town, perhaps high on a hill or in the center of a square, you're likely to spot an old courthouse. These stately buildings are rich in history, appealing to look at, and becoming scarcer and scarcer as modern buildings replace them. Although some historic courthouses are no longer used for their original purpose, a good number of these older buildings still remain in north Georgia. It's interesting to get out and take a look at them. Many have historical markers telling a bit about their history and that of the county.

LOCATION
This book covers 22 of Georgia's 159 counties. Each county has a courthouse in the town known as the county seat.

SEASON
Year-round

TIME ALLOWANCE
Anywhere from a quick stop to several hours if the building houses a museum.

COST
Free

BRING ALONG
Camera, genealogical questions.

NOTE
If some of your ancestors came from the county and you're looking for genealogical information, the county courthouse can be one of the best places to get started.

Courthouse Trivia

STEPHENS COUNTY (TOCCOA)

This is the original courthouse. Built in 1905, it is one of two originals in north Georgia still in use today.

BANKS COUNTY (HOMER)

This building was begun in 1859 and not completed until 1865. A quick history check explains why it took so long—the builders had to stop and fight the Civil War! This building is the other of two original courthouses still in use today in north Georgia.

HALL COUNTY (GAINESVILLE)

The county's first courthouse was built in 1833. It was later replaced by a brick building, which was destroyed in 1936 by Georgia's worst-ever tornado, which killed 170 people. The present courthouse was built in 1937.

The original Lumpkin County courthouse is now the home of the Dahlonega Gold Museum.

WHITE COUNTY (CLEVELAND)

The original courthouse stands in the center of the square in Cleveland. Built in 1860, it served its original purpose for over 100 years. It now houses an historical museum.

LUMPKIN COUNTY (DAHLONEGA)

Now the Dahlonega Gold Museum, the original courthouse was completed in 1836 at a cost of $6,850. The contractor was paid in gold bullion.

PICKENS COUNTY (JASPER)

The present courthouse is the third in line and was completed in 1949. It is made entirely of Georgia marble, quarried in the county.

BARTOW, WHITFIELD, AND DADE COUNTIES (CARTERSVILLE, DALTON, AND TRENTON)

These counties' former courthouses have a common bond—all three were burned down by Union General William T. Sherman during his Civil War "March to the Sea." This is particularly interesting since Dade County seceded from the state of Georgia at the outbreak of the war and was actually a part of the Union during the conflict.

Backroads Touring

You'll see plenty of country churches dotting the landscape.

A rock pile marking the grave of a Cherokee princess is one of the surprises you might find.

Hundreds of miles of roads trace through the coves and over the mountains of north Georgia. Many are designated Georgia highways, while others are simply paved county roads. Sometimes it's fun just to go for a drive in the mountains with no real destination planned; the surprise of a new discovery is what makes the trip. The way to go about it is to pick up a good road map, chart a basic course, and then just follow your nose and see where it goes.

LOCATION
Some of the roads are highlighted to the right. Other than that, the choice is yours.

SEASON
Year-round

TIME ALLOWANCE
As long as you like.

COST
Free

BRING ALONG
Clothes and shoes to get out and walk around in. Binoculars, camera, road map, picnic.

NOTE
Although it does not show all the counties of north Georgia, the Chattahoochee-Oconee National Forest map shows more roadways than just about any other source for Georgia. It can be purchased from the Chattahoochee National Forest headquarters (p. 132) or from the various Forest Service district offices.

GA 180

This is one of north Georgia's most scenic highways. Starting almost at the foot of Brasstown Bald, the road traverses east to west and mostly takes the same route, via the low road, as the Appalachian Trail. You'll pass Vogel State Park and ride through the Sosebee Scenic Area, across Wolfpen Gap, past Lake Winfield Scott, and finally through high rolling farmland, ending in the tiny town of Suches.

GA 60

To drive this road, you'll begin at the huge rock pile nine miles north of Dahlonega on US 19. This large pile of rocks at the intersection of the two roads is said to be the grave of Trahlyta, a Cherokee Indian princess. It is considered good luck to leave a rock atop the pile. Once past it you'll ascend, with beautiful views, to Woody Gap. On the other side you'll pass through Suches, alongside the serene Toccoa River, through beautiful mountain farmland, past Lake Blue Ridge, and, finally, all the way to McCaysville, on the Tennessee line.

GA 136

This long, east-to-west route begins just north of Gainesville on the northern shore of Lake Sidney Lanier. You could easily call this the country store route as you'll pass a good number of them on the drive. Along the way are little towns with the most interesting names: Talking Rock, Resaca, Villanow, Naomi,

Great Roads in North Georgia

LaFayette (pronounced l`FAY-et. "FAY-et" rhymes with "say it" and is said with a slight twang). The road ends on the other side of Lookout Mountain and Cloudland Canyon at the Alabama line just past I-59.

ASKA, NEWPORT, BIG CREEK ROADS

Beginning in Blue Ridge, you'll climb to Deep Gap on Aska Road and then drop down alongside the Toccoa River. Here the road winds parallel to the river and then through quiet mountain farmland. Upon reaching Newport Road you'll turn right and cruise up and over, past rural churches to Big Creek Road. Here you'll turn right again, roll up and down though more farmland, and finally end up in the apple orchards on GA 52 just east of Ellijay.

Horseshoe or hairpin turn? Hairpin turns are so tight the road almost meets itself.

Apple Orchards

orth Georgia is apple country, and in the heart of it all is Ellijay, Georgia's apple capital. Head off on any backroad out of Ellijay and you'll soon be in the middle of an apple orchard. Spring visitors will be greeted with sweet-smelling pink blooms frosting the countryside. Summer visitors will see apples in varying stages of development, and fall visitors will get the best of all—a chance to sample the apples themselves. Pull up at any apple house or roadside stand and you can buy apples by the peck, half bushel, bushel, or just a bag for munching on the spot.

LOCATION
Orchards are scattered throughout the northern counties, with the highest concentration around Ellijay.

SEASON
Depending on the variety, apples are harvested from late August through mid-November. Most trees bloom in mid-April.

TIME ALLOWANCE
For buying apples, give yourself at least an hour to choose an apple house and then sample and select the varieties you like. You can spend several hours to all day driving through the orchards.

COST
Looking and sampling are free. Prices range from about $3 a peck to $14 per bushel.

BRING ALONG
Camera, a sweater in the fall (it can be cool in the apple house), enough cargo space for all those apples, your wallet.

NOTE
Ellijay's annual Apple Festival happens in October (see p.130).

Huge crates of apples explode out of the roadside stores in October.

There's nothing like the taste—and the crunch—of a freshly picked apple on a crisp fall day.

A SHORT HISTORY OF SOUTHERN APPLES

Like everywhere else in America, when settlers first arrived in the South they found no apple trees. To fill the void, apple-loving European pioneers planted seeds themselves, and, over time, extensive orchards of hundreds of thousands of trees dotted the landscape. Most of the apples were used to produce cider.

Modern-day nurseries propagate apple trees by grafting, which results in fruit that grows true to the parent tree. But for over 300 years, trees in the South were typically grown from seed, which resulted in a unique tree from each seed planted. In effect, this made the region a vast experiment station for new apple varieties.

As trees became favorites, their apples were given a name. Eventually, the cream of the crop were grafted and sold by large nurseries. So from the millions of trees, each representing a separate variety, several thousand were given names.

Southern Apples

Only a handful actually became Southern favorites.

OLD SOUTHERN APPLES

By 1928 there were over 1,400 named varieties of apples in the South. Of these, about 90 percent are now considered extinct. Gone are the apples with names like *Sweet Valentine*, *Mason's Stranger*, and *Great Unknown*. While touring some of north Georgia's orchards you'll probably run across some of the survivors, like *Limbertwig*, *Yates*, *Arkansas Black*, *Detroit Red*, and *Winter Banana*.

COMMON VARIETIES OF TODAY

From the thousands of varieties that were once available, the orchard shopper today in north Georgia will have a relative few to choose from. At most stands you'll find the standard *Red Delicious*, *Golden Delicious*, *Rome Beauty*, *Gala*, *Granny Smith*, *Mutsu*, and *Stayman Winesap*. These varieties are the descendants of great Southern apples of old.

THE FIRST COMMERCIAL ORCHARD

The first commercial orchard in Georgia was planted by H.R. Straight in Cornelia in 1895. He was soon joined by Colonel J. D. Fort of Rabun County. Others followed, and the industry grew to create north Georgia's famous apple-growing legacy.

Dahlonega Gold Museum

The Dahlonega Gold Museum was once the home of a US mint.

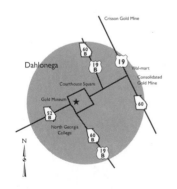

Restrooms (across street)
Handicapped Access

In 1828 gold was "discovered" in the north Georgia mountains and sparked America's first major gold rush. At one point over 70 mines operated in the area surrounding Dahlonega. The old courthouse in Dahlonega, at one time a US mint, now serves as a gold museum. Here, via audio and visual displays, you can learn all about gold mining in north Georgia. The highlight is an excellent 15-minute film in which local folks from mining families divulge their rich heritage and personal experience with Georgia gold.

LOCATION
The old courthouse in the center of the square in downtown Dahlonega.
706-864-2257
www.ngeorgia.com/parks/dahlonega.html

SEASON
Year-round (closed Thanksgiving, Christmas, and New Year's Day)

TIME ALLOWANCE
About an hour

COST
Adults: $2.50
Children: $1.50 (under 5, free)

BRING ALONG
Questions, camera.

NOTE
This is an excellent stop to make before you give gold panning a try at one of the local mines (p. 120).

GOLD WAS DISCOVERED LONG BEFORE IT WAS "DISCOVERED"

The fact that there was gold in the hills of north Georgia was known long before whites ever arrived. Cherokees routinely panned for the yellow metal in the upper reaches of the Chattahoochee River. In the 1540s Hernando de Soto visited the region in search of gold and left behind Spanish miners who formed small settlements that remained for nearly 200 years. Eventually, the Spanish were driven out of Georgia, but mining continued on a very small scale until it was finally rediscovered in White County by Frank Logan in 1828.

PUBLICIZED DISCOVERY SPARKS A MAJOR GOLD RUSH

Shortly after Logan's discovery, gold was reported in a number of locations in north Georgia, including the area surrounding Dahlonega. By 1830 more than 300 ounces of gold were being produced per day. Dahlonega was a boom town, and "gold fever" brought miners from all over the world. The town had a major road leading to it, a post office, and a newspaper. One hotel was owned by John C. Calhoun, then vice president of the United States.

THE LAND WAS TAKEN FROM THE CHEROKEE

In the 1830s, most of the land in north Georgia was still owned by the Cherokee Nation. For some time whites had been plotting a way to acquire the land, and gold was just the catalyst they needed to get broad public support. Within ten years of the "discovery," the Cherokee were forcibly removed to the west (see Trail of Tears, p. 99).

America's First Gold Rush

AS ONE RUSH ENDS, ANOTHER BEGINS

In 1838 so much gold was being produced that a branch of the US mint was built in Dahlonega. Upon completion of the mint, however, the amount of gold produced went into decline. Gold was discovered in California in 1849, and many of the miners left. Gold mining continued, but on a much smaller scale.

STREETS OF GOLD

Ever heard it said that the streets of Atlanta are paved with gold? It's truer than you think. Sand from north Georgia for concrete, cement, and asphalt frequently has measurable amounts of gold, and much of it shows up in the state capital.

Natural Wonders

Almost every area of the country has some feature that stands out as a wonder of nature. North Georgia has some amazing examples. Look for stalactites and stalagmites in a cave, then splash in a public swimming pool filled with spring water that flows from the cave's entrance in—you guessed it—Cave Springs. Explore the depths of two deep trenches in the earth, both carved by rivers, at Cloudland Canyon and Tallulah Gorge. And speaking of rivers, don't forget the famous Chattooga, one of the first waterways designated under the 1968 Wild and Scenic Rivers Act. Explore its waters by whitewater raft, or hike the trails along its protected banks.

WATERFALLS, BALDS, CAVES, AND CANYONS

And then there are the waterfalls … Take your pick between Amicalola Falls, the second highest falls in the East; Anna Ruby Falls, which is actually two falls in one; or the mighty Bull Sluice on the Chattooga River. There are many more, and most are accessible by footpath.

Last but certainly not least, visit spectacular Brasstown Bald, where you can take in the view and learn how a wasted forest can be reclaimed.

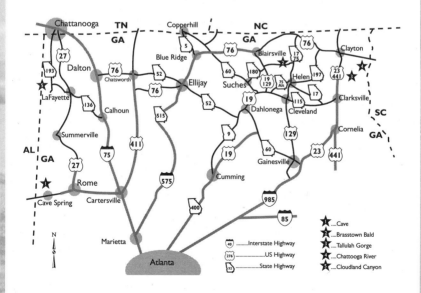

Brasstown Bald

There is a 360° view from the top of the observation deck.

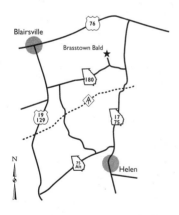

Restrooms
Gift Shop
Picnic Tables
Handicapped Access

At 4,784 feet, Brasstown Bald is Georgia's highest peak. Located just outside of the Brasstown Bald Wilderness, this mountaintop is easily accessible by car—that is, all but the last (steep) half-mile, which is a paved foot trail that gains 500 feet. At the very top is an impressive visitors center, where on a *very* clear day you can see the Atlanta skyline more than 100 miles away as well as a 360° view of the surrounding Blue Ridge. Indoors, the interpretive center covers everything from the early days of logging, to the natural history of the mountain, to a history of the Forest Service. There's even a small theater with a film highlighting the four seasons on Brasstown Bald.

LOCATION
From Helen, take GA 17/75 north over Unicoi Gap, then turn left on GA 180. Go 5 miles and turn onto GA 180 Spur. It's 3 miles to the top. 706-896-2556.

SEASON
Daily: Memorial Day–October 31. Weekends only: early spring and late fall (depending on weather).

TIME ALLOWANCE
2–3 hours

COST
$3.00 parking fee.
$1.50 for shuttle bus to top to avoid the hike.

BRING ALONG
Camera, binoculars, sturdy walking shoes, and field guides to trees and wildflowers.

NOTE
Dazzling wildflowers bloom in late May and June along the hike to the top. A shuttle concession runs a small bus to the very top for those who are unable, or do not care, to walk.

FARMERS TURNED TO LOG-GING AS THEIR CASH CROP

In the years preceding and just after the American Civil War most folks in north Georgia lived by cultivating the land. For many in these rugged mountains, it was a hard way to survive. With the arrival of logging toward the end of the 19th century, folks began to realize that they could make a better living by first selling off most of their land to logging companies and then going to work as loggers themselves, clearing the forest of trees.

THE CROSSCUT SAW REVOLU-TIONIZED THE INDUSTRY

Early logging methods were pretty slow going. With a stone broad axe, a logger did well to cut down and prepare one big tree per day. With a steel one, it was not much quicker. With the invention of the two-person crosscut saw near the turn of the century, it was possible to fell and prepare close to 50 trees a day. This one invention modernized the timber industry. By 1910 the South led the nation in lumber production, and the mills in the mountains of north Georgia were the biggest producers at 350 million board feet per year. The largest mill in the eastern US was located in Helen.

ALL THIS PRODUCTION DID NOT COME WITHOUT A PRICE

Early loggers took the largest and best trees in the forest. Only the sickly and damaged trees remained,

Logging at the Turn of the Century

leaving poor breeding stock for future generations of trees. To get the logs to the mills, loggers sent the great trees tearing down the steep mountainsides. Anything in their way was ripped from its roots, leaving the path open for erosion and

disease. More trees meant more money, and before long there was little left on the hillsides.

Sturdy, narrow gauge railways were constructed deep into the mountains to haul out the logs. The steam locomotives frequently bellowed embers into the air, only to have them settle into the ravaged forest. Wildfires were frequent and devastating. If not for the efforts of forest rangers in the 1920s and the Civilian Conservation Corps in the 1930s, the forests of north Georgia might never have recovered to their beauty of today.

Tallulah Gorge

The interpretive center offers a bird watching area.

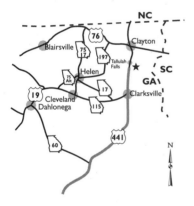

Store
Camping
Restrooms
Picnic Tables
Interpretive Center
Handicapped Access

Millions of years ago, the Tallulah River carved a 600-foot-deep, three-mile-wide trench in the earth known today as Tallulah Gorge. Its impressive cliffs can be viewed from observation points on several short hiking trails along the east rim within the Tallulah Gorge State Park. Hiking trails also lead down into the gorge itself.

Until 1914 the river ran freely through this gorge over a series of six waterfalls. Today, the Tallulah River is held up by a series of dams along much of its course. On selected weekends, however, the river is let loose again for all to see and hear, and to give whitewater kayakers an opportunity to test their skills against its awesome power.

LOCATION
On US 441, 15 miles south of Clayton.
706-754-7970
www.ngeorgia.com/parks/tallulah.html

SEASON
Hiking trails and the Jane Hurt Yarn Interpretive Center are open year-round. See festival information (p. 129) for water release dates.

TIME ALLOWANCE
1–2 hours for visitor center and to view the gorge. Half to all day to hike the trails.

COST
$4 Georgia State Park pass required.

BRING ALONG
Camera, binoculars, walking or hiking shoes.

NOTE
Mountain bikers should note that the state park has a designated bike trail which descends to Lake Tugaloo. It stays away from the rim of the gorge.

Tallulah Gorge's Most Famous Human Event

THE WALK ACROSS TALLULAH GORGE

It was 93° the day the 65-year-old Wallenda mounted the 1,000-foot, two-inch steel cable to begin his walk. Using a 36-pound balancing pole and wearing soft leather shoes, he took 541 steps and less than 18 minutes to cross the gorge, including two separate headstands done 750 feet above the river. One headstand was in memory of family and fellow troupe members who had died in a fall during a performance in 1962. The second, he said, was "for the boys in Vietnam."

Although Wallenda had performed many other "skywalks," crossing wires stretched between high rise buildings and across stadiums like the Astrodome, his walk across Tallulah Gorge was his most famous. Eight years later, he fell to his death while performing a promotional highwire walk in San Juan, Puerto Rico. He was 73.

A HISTORY OF SPECTACLE

Tallulah Gorge has attracted visitors for hundreds of years, but its most spectacular event in recent human history occurred on July 18, 1970. On that day, journalists from across America and Europe, along with 35,000 spectators, gathered to watch high-wire artist Karl Wallenda walk across the gorge on a tightrope.

THE FLYING WALLENDAS

The famous "Flying Wallendas" troupe had been a headliner for the Ringling Brothers, Barnum and Bailey Circus in the 1930s and '40s. Wallenda and his family perfected the seven-person, three-level pyramid highwire act that became a showstopper. He was used to working without a net, and had even performed during an earthquake without mishap.

Chattooga River

Whitewater rafters enjoy a peaceful stretch of river.

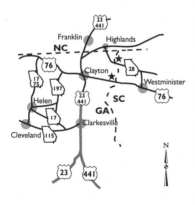

Restrooms
Handicapped Access

 ne of our first national Wild and Scenic Rivers, the Chattooga flows along Georgia's extreme northeast border, adjoining South Carolina. Its 40-mile length is not only very wild and very scenic, it is home to some of the most challenging whitewater in the US. As you might expect, that makes it popular for rafting, canoeing, and kayaking. It's also a choice hiking destination. Many folks come just to see the beauty of the river itself or to watch the boaters challenge the rapids.

As a wild and scenic river, the Chattooga is protected from development within a quarter-mile of its banks. Except for two highway crossings, access to the river is by foot trail only. Some of these trails take you to rapids with names like Bull Sluice, Woodall Shoals, and Seven Foot Falls.

LOCATION
East and northeast of Clayton. Main access points are on US 76 and GA 28.

SEASON
Commercial rafting: March–October. Other uses: year-round.

TIME ALLOWANCE
As long as you like.

COST
See p. 44 for whitewater rafting fees. Some parking areas charge a small fee.

BRING ALONG
Camera, binoculars, walking shoes or hiking boots, snacks or a portable picnic.

NOTE
Some of the sights in the area are only reachable by bumpy and dusty dirt roads.

THE 1968 WILD AND SCENIC RIVERS ACT

It is hereby declared to be the policy of the United States that certain selected rivers of the Nation which, with their immediate environments, possess outstandingly remarkable scenic, recreational, geologic, fish and wildlife, historic, cultural, or other similar values, shall be preserved in free-flowing condition, and that they and their immediate environments shall be protected for the benefit and enjoyment of present and future generations. The Congress declares that the established national policy of dam and other construction at appropriate sections of the rivers of the United States needs to be complemented by a policy that would preserve other selected rivers or sections thereof in their free-flowing condition to protect the water quality of such rivers and to fulfill other vital national conservation purposes.

Hiking trails offer great views of the river from above.

Wild & Scenic Rivers

CHATTOOGA RIVER CLASSIFIED AS WILD AND SCENIC

Georgia is fortunate to have one river included in the national Wild and Scenic Rivers Act—the Chattooga. In fact, it was one of the earliest rivers to gain such a designation, receiving its status on May 10, 1974. Along its course from Cashiers, NC, to Lake Tugaloo, 39.8 miles are classified as "Wild," 2.5 miles are classified as "Scenic," and 14.6 miles are classified as "Recreational."

WHAT DO THE CLASSIFICATIONS MEAN?

Wild river areas are rivers or sections of rivers that are free of impoundments and generally inaccessible except by trail, with watersheds or shorelines essentially primitive, and waters unpolluted. These represent vestiges of primitive America.

Scenic river areas are rivers or sections of rivers that are free of impoundments, with shorelines or watersheds still largely primitive, and shorelines largely undeveloped but accessible in places by roads.

Recreational river areas are rivers or sections of rivers that are readily accessible by road or railroad, that may have some development along their shorelines, and that may have undergone some impoundment or diversion in the past.

Cave Spring Cave

The cave entrance looks like a castle gateway.

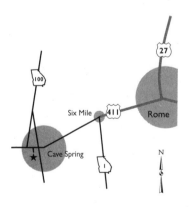

Restrooms
Picnic Tables
Handicapped Access

 ometimes you can find caves in the oddest places. This one, from which a cool stream flows, has a town built around it and gave the town its name: Cave Spring. The cave itself goes several hundred yards back into the hillside. A stone passageway leads the visitor through a narrow opening, where at one point you'll need to duck down, as the ceiling is only five feet high. In the back, the cave opens into a high-ceilinged room. From here, more precarious routes lead to other points in the cave. It is well lit and maintains a temperature of 56° regardless of the time of year.

LOCATION
Rolater Park in the heart of Cave Spring. 706-777-8439.

SEASON
Memorial Day to Labor Day, 11 am – 4 pm.

TIME ALLOWANCE
20 minutes to a half hour for the cave itself.

COST
$1 (3 and under, free)

BRING ALONG
Walking shoes, camera, jugs for water, picnic, swimsuit for pool next door.

NOTE
You can drink the water right where it flows from the cave. Many people like to fill water jugs here. A small pond here is full of trout, and you can buy fish feed at the cave entrance for 25¢ a bag. Just downstream is the Cave Spring Pool (p. 52). There is a $3 rental fee for picnic tables in the park.

Stalactites, Stalagmites ... What's the Difference?

FIRST, WHAT ARE THEY?

Stalactites and stalagmites are the two best known forms of *speleothem* (mineral deposit formations), which occur in caves throughout the world. In the Cave Spring Cave you'll see a number of them, along with other forms of speleothems like *columns, drapery, flowstone,* and *helictites.* Speleothems are formed when mineral-rich water entering the cave crystallizes.

TELLING THE DIFFERENCE

So how do you tell a stalactite from a stalagmite? A stalactite hangs from the ceiling and looks like an earthen icicle. A stalagmite rises from the floor like a pillar. One funny little way to remember it is this: *A stalactite is tight to the ceiling; a stalagmite might reach the ceiling.* Actually, the mineral-rich water dripping from the end of the stalactite forms the stalagmite. When the two eventually meet, a column is formed. You'll see a few of these in the cave as well. Minerals in the water determine the color of speleothems; in the Cave Spring Cave they are a reddish-brown.

FINDING OTHER SPELEOTHEMS

Once you've spotted the obvious stalactites and stalagmites, take a look around and see if you can identify other speleothems. A look along the ceiling may reveal some drapery (thin sheets of hanging rock). A visual search of the tight spaces may reward you with some helictites (strangely twisted cylinders). Check along the walls for flowstone. This develops where a thin sheet of mineralized water flows along the wall and sometimes across the floor.

FASCINATING AND DANGEROUS PLACES

Caves are fascinating, but they can be dangerous places. Scientists who study caves are known as *speleologists. Spelunkers,* who explore unknown caves, do so at great risk. It is best to leave cave exploration to the experts. Never venture into an unknown cave alone or without proper training.

Cloudland Canyon

Clifftop overlooks offer great views of the canyon.

loudland Canyon is an 800-foot gorge carved over many centuries by Sitton Gulch Creek. The entire area is encompassed by Cloudland Canyon State Park, which contains a campground, a picnic area, cabins, and a network of trails. Probably the two main attractions are the views of Lookout Mountain from the bluffs above the canyon and the trails, which are excellent for day hikes. Two beautiful waterfalls are accessible by trail in the canyon itself.

LOCATION
On GA 136, eight miles east of Trenton and I-59, and 18 miles west of LaFayette.
706-657-4050
www.ngeorgia.com/parks/cloudland.html

SEASON
Year–round

TIME ALLOWANCE
Anywhere from one hour to view the canyon to a weekend camping trip.

COST
$2 park pass required Thursday–Tuesday. Wednesdays are free.

BRING ALONG
Camera, binoculars, hiking shoes, extra layers (in cooler weather), rain gear, picnic.

NOTE
The trails in Cloudland Canyon are highlighted in the appendix under suggested day hikes on p. 137.

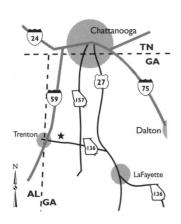

Store
Camping
Restrooms
Picnic Tables
Handicapped Access

Canyons of the South

YES, CANYONS EXIST IN THE SOUTHERN US

For no small reason, canyons in the US are mostly associated with the West. We think of giants like Bryce Canyon, Canyon de Chelly, Canyonlands National Park, and, of course, the biggest of all—the Grand Canyon. Many folks don't associate canyons with the South, let alone north Georgia. Yet they *are* found here, albeit on a somewhat smaller (but no less grand) scale.

TWO OF GEORGIA'S CANYONS ARE FOUND IN THE UPPER CORNERS OF THE STATE

You'll find two canyons in north Georgia: Cloudland Canyon and Tallulah Gorge. Cloudland is located in the far northwest corner, and Tallulah is found in the far northeastern part of the state. Neither are very large as canyons go, but they do exhibit classic steep walls and deep valleys. Farther south in Georgia is Providence Canyon, a remarkable example of erosion at work.

MORE CANYONS ARE FOUND THROUGHOUT THE SOUTH

Just over the line from northwest Georgia is Alabama's Little River Canyon. Touted as one of the deepest canyons east of the Mississippi, this one is 26 miles long. In North Carolina, Nantahala Gorge and Linville Gorge are both ancient and famous—the latter remote, the former more accessible. In Tennessee, the Big South Fork of the Cumberland River Gorge is now entirely contained in a national recreation area. Finally, there's the Grand Canyon of the East—the New River Gorge in West Virginia.

SOUTHERN CANYONS ARE NOT TO BE MISSED

Experiencing any of these canyons is not altogether different than visiting their Western counterparts. All have hiking trails leading into and out of them, views from the rims are almost always spectacular, and several contain challenging white-water rivers in their depths. They may not be as big or as well known, but the canyons of the South are important parts of the landscape you won't want to miss.

Tallulah is a steep-walled gorge with numerous waterfalls within.

Waterfalls

The hike to Dukes Creek Falls is well worth it.

t is a given that the mountains of north Georgia are full of waterfalls. Almost every stream at some point takes a freefall off the side of a mountain. After a heavy rain, waterfalls seem to sprout right out of the rocks. Many of these falls are quite spectacular, and some are pretty famous, with entire state parks named after them. You may enjoy discovering those hidden falls way back in the wilderness, or you may prefer the ones accessible by car. Whatever your choice, there are plenty of them.

LOCATION
Almost anywhere you go in these mountains you will find waterfalls, with each region boasting its most famous ones. See the opposite page for some of the most popular.

SEASON
Year–round

TIME ALLOWANCE
As long as you like.

COST
Most are free, but visiting some of the more popular ones requires paying a small parking fee.

BRING ALONG
Camera, binoculars, walking shoes, maps and guidebooks.

NOTE
Climbing on or near waterfalls is very dangerous, and every year someone is seriously hurt or killed taking a foolish risk. Many popular falls have warning signs and some are enclosed by fences, but in the backcountry there are no signs or fences. No matter how tempting it may be to climb them, don't do it!

The view from atop Amicalola Falls is one of Georgia's best.

AMICALOLA FALLS

Located in Amicalola Falls State Park on GA 52 between Ellijay and Dahlonega, the seven cascades of the falls total 729 feet. They can be viewed from the bottom by way of a hiking trail or from the top, where a platform bridge takes you right to the brink. The view from here is one of the best in north Georgia.

ANNA RUBY FALLS

You'll find Anna Ruby Falls just outside Unicoi State Park and north of Helen. This is actually two falls in one—a 150-foot fall from Curtis Creek and a 50-foot fall from York Creek merge here to form Smith Creek. A 0.4-mile paved trail takes you to the site.

BULL SLUICE

Just upstream of where US 76 crosses the Chattooga River east of Clayton on the GA/SC border is the mighty Bull Sluice. This impressive waterfall is navigated daily by whitewater enthusiasts in rafts, canoes, and kayaks—quite a sight to see. A half-mile trail on the SC side of the river leads to the falls.

TALLULAH FALLS

Within the Tallulah Gorge on US 441 south of Clayton are a series of waterfalls collectively called Tallulah Falls. The falls can be viewed from observation platforms along the rim of the gorge in Tallulah Falls State Park, or for the more adventure-

Some of North Georgia's Most Famous Falls

some, close up by way of several fairly difficult footpaths leading into the gorge itself.

KEOWN FALLS

Aside from the falls inside Cloudland Canyon, Keown Falls is one of the few falls in northwest Georgia. It is found along the Ridge and Valley Scenic Byway (p. 56) on Pocket Road. A foot trail leads to the falls, which are small but attractive. Be aware that during dry weather the falls are also dry. A sign will let you know before you begin your hike.

DESOTO FALLS

Located on US 129 north of Dahlonega and south of the Appalachian Trail, Desoto Falls refers to a number of falls within the Desoto Falls Scenic Area. The falls are reached by a foot trail.

Native American History

Long before European explorers and settlers arrived in the New World, north Georgia was inhabited by native people. The earliest evidence exists in ancient remains of the Mississippian culture, whose legacy can be seen at the Etowah Indian Mounds and at Track Rock, whose mysterious petroglyphs are undeciphered to this day. And historians are still wondering about what look like the ruins of a huge stone wall atop Fort Mountain.

More recently, the Cherokee Nation flourished here. Today, at New Echota, the seat of 18th-century Cherokee culture, a reconstructed outdoor museum illustrates the sophistication of native government, communications, and everyday living before the Cherokees were forced to give up their lands and march west into new territory.

THE HOMES OF CHEROKEE CHIEFS STILL STAND

North Georgia is also rich in the history of individual Cherokee leaders. You can visit the homes of James Vann, Major Ridge, and the most famous of all, John Ross, whose 38-year tenure as principal chief of his nation spanned both its highest point and its lowest—the Cherokee Trail of Tears.

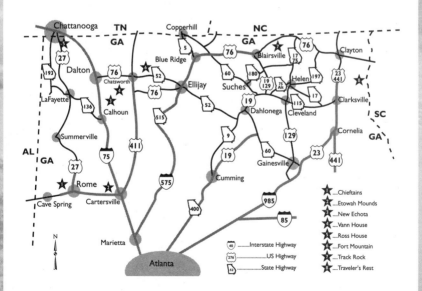

★....Chieftains
★....Etowah Mounds
★....New Echota
★....Vann House
★....Ross House
★....Fort Mountain
★....Track Rock
★....Traveler's Rest

40 ....Interstate Highway
276 ....US Highway
52 ....State Highway

Etowah Indian Mounds

Imagine what this mound looked like 500 years ago.

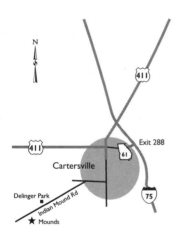

Restrooms
Handicapped Access

This is the closest thing to the Great Pyramids that north Georgia has to offer. Built over the course of 500 years from AD 1000 to 1500, the mounds are an impressive sight. There are three in all—the largest is 63 feet high and covers three acres. Wooden steps lead to the top of each mound, where you will find an excellent view of the surrounding countryside, including the Etowah River, which boasts the remains of an ancient Indian fish trap. The grounds includes an excellent interpretive museum.

LOCATION
6 miles southwest of Cartersville. From I-75, take Exit 288 onto GA 61. Go through town to Indian Mounds Road. For information, call 770-387-3747.

SEASON
Year-round: Tuesday–Saturday, 9 am – 5 pm; Sunday, 2:00–5:30 pm.
Closed Mondays and major holidays.

TIME ALLOWANCE
1–3 hours

COST
Adults: $3
Children: $2 (under 5, free)

BRING ALONG
Camera, binoculars, warm clothes if the weather is cool, sunscreen on a sunny day, water bottle.

NOTE
This is very much an outside activity which requires about a half mile of walking with little or no shade. No picnicking is available at the mounds, but Delinger Park just down the road has plenty of sheltered tables.

The Mound Builders

WHO WERE THE MOUND BUILDERS?

The mound builders lived in North America from about AD 800 to the arrival of European explorers. Those who made their home alongside the Etowah in north Georgia were members of the Mississippian culture, a group that covered a large part of the continent within the Mississippi River watershed. These people enjoyed an intricate system of trading, were accomplished craftspeople, and practiced sophisticated religious beliefs.

WHY WERE THE MOUNDS BUILT?

The people at Etowah and at other sites were governed by chief priests. The priests lived atop earthen mounds overlooking a central plaza. As each chief died, the temple was destroyed and then covered by a layer of earth before another temple was built for the next chief priest. In this process, the mounds were built higher and higher over the course of centuries. Smaller

mounds within the area would have been the homes of lesser priests, and their social standing determined how close to the mounds they were allowed to live.

HOW WERE THE MOUNDS BUILT?

In prehistoric times there were no great earth-moving tools such as we have today. Modern bulldozers and heavy equipment could build a mound like the ones at Etowah in a day. Instead, the mound builders relied on small woven baskets, carried in their hands or on their backs, to move the dirt. Off to the side of the village, a pit, called a borrow pit, would slowly be dug as the earth was moved from there to the mound. Who knows the number of trips between pit and mound that must have been made during construction.

The visitor center at Etowah is located by the old borrow pit. As you walk out of the building and onto the site, imagine carrying a basketful of earth. Carry it to the top of the highest mound and dump it there. Now imagine doing it all day, every day for the rest of your life, and you get a picture of a major activity of the mound builders.

Chief Vann House

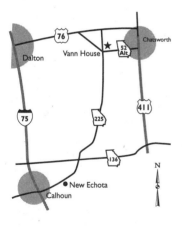

The elegant home of Chief James Vann was designed and built by Moravians whom Vann helped bring to this country.

Standing on an open knoll, the three-story brick plantation house built by Chief James Vann in 1804 is an impressive sight. With its colorful decor, cantilevered staircase, and captivating view, it's no wonder it is known as the "showplace of the Cherokee Nation." A guided tour of the house reveals life as it was lived by a wealthy Cherokee chief and his family. Not only will you see a great collection of antiques, but also you will learn that like most Cherokees, Chief Vann lived a life far different from our stereotype of the hostile savage.

LOCATION
Just west of Chatsworth at the junction of GA 52A and GA 225.
706-695-2598 or VannHouse@alltel.net

SEASON
Year-round: Tuesday–Saturday, 9 am – 5 pm; Sunday, 2:00–5:30 pm.
Closed Monday and major holidays.

TIME ALLOWANCE
45 minutes – I hour

COST
Adults: $2.50
Children 6+: $1.50 (under 6, free)

BRING ALONG
Camera, questions.

NOTE
The Chief Vann House is only about 15 miles north of New Echota (p. 98). Both can be seen easily in a morning or afternoon. Neither, however, has picnic facilities, and the closest available are on I-75 or in Chatsworth, so plan your outing accordingly.

Restrooms
Handicapped Access

THE CHEROKEES WERE NOT YOUR STEREOTYPICAL AMERICAN INDIANS

The stereotypical American Indian lived in a teepee, wore a buckskin breechcloth, rode a pony bareback, took scalps, hunted with a bow and arrow, wore a headdress full of feathers, and carried a tomahawk. At least, this is the impression left to us by some American painters, novelists, and moviemakers. Certainly, many tribes did do some of these things, and the Cherokee of Georgia probably exhibited a few as well. But to accurately envision a Cherokee of around the year 1800, we must turn to the facts.

THE TYPICAL CHEROKEE LIVED MUCH THE SAME AS THE EARLY WHITE SETTLER

The Cherokees, impressed by the ways of the "white man," gradually began to adopt their ways. The typical Cherokee at the end of the 18th century lived much the same as the early white settler—in a log cabin surrounded by a vegetable garden, a smokehouse, a corn crib, and other food-processing buildings. He dressed in similar clothes and traded regularly at white-owned stores.

SOME CHEROKEES WERE VERY WEALTHY

A few Cherokees accumulated great wealth. They lived in stately homes, held vast amounts of land, and owned black slaves. Chief James

The Cherokee Nation

Vann was one of these, and the stately Vann House serves as a reminder of this bygone era in Cherokee history. Another well-to-do Cherokee was Chief John Ross, who was at one time a merchant, a postmaster, and a planter owning twenty slaves. Ross's main adversary, Major Ridge, owned a profitable ferry service and lands as well.

THE CHEROKEE NATION WAS SEPARATE FROM THAT OF THE UNITED STATES

The Cherokee Nation was separate from that of the United States, with its own formal system of government. Its constitution, adopted in 1827, was very similar to the US Constitution, and its government was divided into executive, legislative, and judicial branches. The legislature was made up of the National Committee and National Council, and the executive power rested with a sole individual—the Principal Chief. Members of the General Council ruled the courts and elected the Principal Chief.

The seven-pointed star represented the seven branches of the nation.

New Echota

Tribal decisions were made at the council house at New Echota.

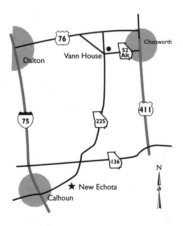

Restrooms
Handicapped Access

New Echota was the last capital of the Cherokee Nation before the great "Trail of Tears." This thriving community had stores, council houses, and its own newspaper. After the removal to Oklahoma in 1838, the town fell into ruin and finally was plowed under to cultivate fields of cotton. Beginning in 1954, a group of archeologists reconstructed the town plan. The state of Georgia has restored the one remaining building and built fine replicas of others. In the museum, you can view a 15-minute film about the history of New Echota and the Cherokee Nation, hear the Cherokee language being spoken, and see relics of a lost way of life.

LOCATION
On GA 225 north of Calhoun.
Take Exit 317 from I-75.
706-624-1321
www.innerx.net/~newechota

SEASON
Year-round: Tuesday–Saturday, 9 am – 5 pm; Sunday, 2:00–5:30 pm.
Closed Monday and major holidays

TIME ALLOWANCE
1½ – 2½ hours

COST
Adults: $2.50
Children 6+: $1.50 (under 6, free)

BRING ALONG
Camera, walking shoes, sun hat and sunscreen, water bottle.

NOTE
Touring the town, you may walk a mile or so in the open, so be prepared for the weather. The Chief Vann House (p. 96) is only about 15 miles north.

The Trail of Tears

GOLD- AND LAND-HUNGRY WHITES DESPERATELY WANT CHEROKEE LANDS

As the United States grew, more and more land was needed to satisfy the growing population of settlers. Unfortunately for the Native American tribes who owned the majority of the land, white settlers' needs took precedence over land ownership. This was certainly the case with the Cherokee Nation in north Georgia. Georgians wanted the Cherokees' land, and with the discovery of gold near Dahlonega in 1830 (p. 77), the demand escalated. Surveys were conducted and lotteries were held to give Cherokee lands to whites. The Cherokees, led by their chief John Ross, took their case to the Supreme Court of the United States. Though they won in court, they lost their land in Georgia.

ILLEGAL TREATY ENDS HOPES OF CHEROKEES REMAINING IN THEIR HOMELANDS

A small faction led by Major Ridge (p. 101) believed the Cherokee Nation would be better off if they did remove to the west. In December of 1835 this minority faction signed a treaty with the US accepting the terms of removal. The majority of the Cherokees, including their chief, opposed this illegal treaty vehemently and worked diligently to reverse it. Their attempts failed. It was ratified in May 1836 by the US Senate by a one-vote margin. Still, the majority of the Cherokees did not believe they would really be forced to leave. As we now know, they were wrong.

ONE FIFTH OF ENTIRE CHEROKEE NATION DIES DURING FORCED REMOVAL

Two years later, in May of 1838, the forced removal of the Cherokee to the western territories began. It was not one of the United States' finer moments. Families were separated, people were dragged from their homes, and their property was looted. Members of the tribe were rounded up and imprisoned in a series of stockades throughout the territory. Then over the terrible winter of 1838–39, they were forced to march— many in ragged clothing and malnourished—for over 800 miles. Some went by barge, others by wagon, but the vast majority went on foot. Nearly a fifth of the entire population of the Cherokee Nation—over 4,000 souls—died en route. This death march was to go down in history as "the Trail of Tears."

Chieftains Museum

ituated on the banks of the Oostanaula River and nearly in the heart of Rome, the Chieftains Museum is the former home of Major Ridge, a leading figure in the signing of the agreement to the removal of the Cherokee. Now surrounded by industry and development, his white clapboard home once sat on the edge of the wilderness. What a difference 200 years can make! Inside are exhibits which describe Ridge's life and general Cherokee history.

LOCATION
In Rome, on Riverside Parkway between GA 53 Spur and US 27.
706-291-9494
chmuseum@roman.net

SEASON
Year-round: Tuesday–Saturday, 10 am – 4 pm; Closed Sunday, Monday, and major holidays.

TIME ALLOWANCE
1–2 hours

COST RANGE
Adults: $3.00
Students: $1.50
Seniors: $2.00

BRING ALONG
Questions, Cherokee history books.

NOTE
The museum is a good option for a rainy day. Also, it is very close to Berry College (p. 66) and a few miles upstream of the Lock and Dam Park (p. 64).

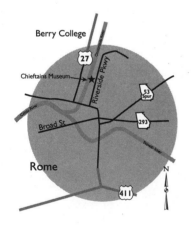

Restrooms
Handicapped Access

RIDGE BELIEVED REMOVAL BEST FOR CHEROKEE NATION

During the time leading up to the "Trail of Tears," Major Ridge led the faction of Cherokees who thought removal was the best alternative for their nation. They sincerely believed that the only salvation for their people lay in moving beyond the sphere of white influence. For a time, they believed in and supported their chief, John Ross. But it did not take long for the Ridge faction and the Ross party to split widely on this matter. The Ross party was firmly set on remaining in the Cherokee homeland.

THE TREATY OF NEW ECHOTA IS SIGNED WHILE THE CHIEF IS AWAY IN WASHINGTON

In December 1835, while Chief John Ross was away in Washington, Major Ridge and other leaders of his faction came together at New Echota to meet with Federal Commissioner John F. Schermerhorn. Although no elected leaders of the tribe were present, an agreement-to-removal treaty was drawn up and signed. According to the treaty, for the sum of $5 million the entire Cherokee Nation would give

Major Ridge and the Treaty of New Echota

Major Ridge

up its lands in the East and remove to a tract of land in the Indian Territory (now part of Oklahoma).

"I HAVE SIGNED MY DEATH WARRANT"

It is generally believed that as Major Ridge signed the Treaty of New Echota, he said, "I have signed my death warrant." Whether he said it or not, it became true for him and a number of other prominent signers. Over a period of two days in June 1839, these men, now in the Indian Territory, were ambushed or dragged from their homes by members of their own tribe, and slain.

Fort Mountain

 tanding like a sentinel overlooking the Great Valley, Fort Mountain is easy to recognize. High atop the mountain is Fort Mountain State Park, with all the state park amenities you'd expect, along with hiking, biking, and horse trails. An ancient stone wall gives the mountain its name and ties it to Native American heritage. The 855-foot wall was built a very long time ago and no one knows by whom, although there are a number of theories. Hike out to the wall and up to the stone tower and observation deck. After giving it a good look, decide which one you think best explains the wall's true origin.

Fort Mountain towers over north Georgia's Great Valley.

LOCATION
Atop Fort Mountain on GA 52, halfway between Chatsworth and Ellijay.
706-695-2621
www.ngeorgia.com/parks/fort.html

SEASON
Year–round

TIME ALLOWANCE
1–2 hours to see wall and overlook.

COST
$2 park pass required. Wednesdays are free.

BRING ALONG
Comfortable walking clothing, sturdy shoes, camera, sun protection, water, a picnic.

NOTE
The hike up to the wall is not too long, but it requires ascending a trail and stone steps. Getting to the tower and overlook platform requires more steps. Depending on how you go from the tower, the hike down to the platform is either steep and rocky or longer but more gradual.

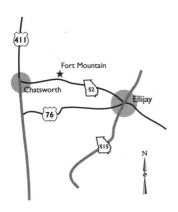

Camping
Restrooms
Picnic Tables
Handicapped Access

MORE THAN JUST A PILE OF ROCKS

To date, no one has definitely established the origin of the stone wall atop Fort Mountain. It certainly has been up there a very long time—long enough that it now resembles a jumble of rocks as much as it does a wall. In fact, if you're not paying attention as you approach it, it's easy to hike right over the top before realizing you've passed it. Once you recognize what you're looking at, however, it becomes clear this is more than just a pile of rocks. The wall follows a straight east-to-west line, with a depression or pit every so often. Near the information signs you'll see what appears to be an entrance.

THE MOST ROMANTIC THEORY

In Cherokee tradition, a legend passed down from their ancient chiefs tells that the mountain was once inhabited by a race of whites with blond hair and blue eyes. The Cherokees referred to them as the "moon-eyed people" because of their keen sight by night and near blindness during the day. Supposedly, the Cherokees dispensed with these people in a great slaughter. The tale is lent support by some historians who believe that a Prince Madoc sailed from Wales to the coast of Alabama in 1170 with 200 people and eleven ships. These people were eventually driven into the north Georgia mountains by Native Americans.

The Mysterious Fort Mountain Wall

THE OTHER THEORIES

Some believe the wall was built in 500 BC by an ancient race of Native Americans who were sun worshippers, which would explain the wall's east-west orientation. Others believe it may have been built by the Cherokees themselves. Still others think it may have been the work of explorer Hernando de Soto.

One of the latest theories is that it was built by Norseman Leif Erikson and is actually the remains of a huge tower. Possible "story stones" found in the area may shed further light on this theory.

Finally, some geologists believe it is the remnants of a horizontal stratum of a hard caprock broken down by time and natural weathering. Take a good look yourself and see which theory you believe.

Much of what remains of the wall is swallowed in the underbrush.

John Ross House

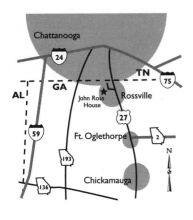

ituated next to Poplar Springs in downtown Rossville, the John Ross House now looks a little out of place. This relic from the past is a classic two-story log dwelling built in 1797. It was the home of John Ross, Principal Chief of the Cherokee Nation. Ross was chief for 38 years, and it was during his tenure that the Cherokee left their homelands and embarked on their forced removal. Ross voluntarily accompanied his people to Oklahoma, where he died at the age of 79. The house is a simple structure and provides a good idea of how a Cherokee chief lived in the early 19th century.

LOCATION
In Rossville, on US 27 just south of the TN/GA border. Take Spring Street one block west to Lake Avenue. Turn right. The house is located in the Chief John Ross Park on the left.

SEASON
The porch and grounds are open year-round 1–5 pm. The house is usually open 1–5 pm (except Wednesday), June – September.

To set up appointments, groups may call ahead to Larry Rose, 706-866-5171, or write: 826 Chickamauga Ave., Rossville, GA 30741.

TIME ALLOWANCE
Exterior: 15–30 minutes
Interior: 1 hour

COST
Free

BRING ALONG
Camera, Cherokee historical information.

THE EARLY LIFE OF JOHN ROSS

Born in 1790 and only one-eighth Cherokee, John Ross was an unlikely prospect to become one of the Cherokee Nation's greatest chiefs. Ross was short, did not speak the Cherokee language well, and was educated by tutors at a private academy. But at his father's trading store where he grew up, Ross favored the more traditional dress and customs of the Cherokees. His Cherokee name as a child was *Tsan Usudi* or "Little John." In adulthood it would change to *Kooweskoowe*, the name of a rare migratory bird. He received a practical knowledge of merchandising and management at the academy and he learned the art of personal persuasion—skills that would last him a lifetime.

A CHEROKEE ADVOCATE AND LEADER

In young adulthood after serving a stint in the military during the Creek Wars, the merchant John Ross became more and more involved in Cherokee politics. What began with a trip to Washington here and there led to his presidency of the Cherokee National Committee. During the period 1815–1828, Ross witnessed the gradual chipping away of the Cherokee lands by the US and state governments. As an influential leader, he was offered money, lands, and prestige to sign various documents that would give the US more Cherokee land. He never signed a single one. In 1828, after the death of Principal Chief

John Ross, Cherokee Chief

Pathkiller, John Ross became chief of the Cherokee. It was a post he would hold until his death in 1866.

LEADING HIS PEOPLE IN THE BEST AND WORST OF TIMES

John Ross's early leadership and then tenure as Principal Chief of the Cherokees spanned an era when their nation saw the pinnacle of its civilization and one when it was plunged into the depths of human suffering. It was clearly the most dynamic period in Cherokee history. In the late 1820s and early 1830s, Cherokee leadership was strong, but the "white man's" quest for land was even stronger. In 1838 the Cherokee were removed to lands in Oklahoma in a forced march that has become known as the "Trail of Tears" (p. 99).

WORKING FOR THE INTEGRITY OF THE CHEROKEE NATION

From the time of the removal until his death in 1866, John Ross worked at every turn to keep his people together, both politically and socially. Only months before he died, he was again in Washington—this time with officials meeting him at his bedside. He was working on yet another treaty to maintain the integrity of the Cherokee Nation.

Track Rock

Steel cages help protect the petroglyphs from vandalism.

Scattered about in the southern Appalachians are signs that people inhabited this region long before whites arrived, and even before the recognized Native American tribes. One such site is Track Rock, where ancient petroglyphs are carved into an outcropping of rock. No one knows for sure what the carvings mean. Maybe this was the junction of an ancient road, and they are "road signs" from the past. Maybe a prehistoric artist was describing a great hunt. It's fun to guess for yourself what they might signify. See if you can identify footprints, bird tracks, crosses, or circles. The rocks are surrounded by metal cages for their protection.

LOCATION
Take Track Rock Road off US 76 between Young Harris and Blairsville. The rocks are found on the west side of the road at Track Rock Gap, with a roadside parking lot just below them.

SEASON
Year-round

TIME ALLOWANCE
30 minutes to an hour

COST RANGE
Free

BRING ALONG
Camera, good walking shoes.

NOTE
If you are making a tour along the Russell/Brasstown Scenic Byway (p. 58), you'll see the sign for Track Rock soon after turning east on GA 180. It makes for a delightful and scenic side trip.

PETROGLYPHS ARE A FORM OF HIEROGLYPHICS

The carvings you see at Track Rock are a form of hieroglyphics known as petroglyphs. In essence, the word *petroglyph* means "rock carving," and most of the time it refers to prehistoric rock carvings. Some believe that the Track Rock images are not just a bunch of drawings on some rocks, but actually hieroglyphics—a form of writing in which picture symbols represent ideas.

THE EGYPTIANS USED HIEROGLYPHICS FOR OVER 3,000 YEARS

Most often, hieroglyphics refer to the ancient writings of Egypt. Egyptians used hieroglyphics for over 3,000 years and developed them from rudimentary carvings in stone to sophisticated writing on a form of paper they invented from a reed plant called papyrus. In the

Ancient Forms of Writing

early 1800s, scholars developed ways to translate Egyptian writing. Other forms of hieroglyphics were used by the Hittites of what is now Turkey and by the Aztecs and Mayans of Central America. Scholars have been able to figure out the writings of the Hittites and Aztecs, but, like the petroglyphs of Track Rock, many of the Mayan hieroglyphics remain a mystery.

PICTURE WRITING WAS USED EXTENSIVELY BY NORTH AMERICAN TRIBES

Many North American tribes used hieroglyphics as well. They drew simple pictures on animal skins, tree bark, and on cave or cliff walls. The pictures might represent the events in an individual's life or a tribe's history.

It was not until a brilliant but illiterate Cherokee by the name of Sequoyah developed what was to become the Cherokee syllabary that any North American tribe had a formal alphabet. It took Sequoyah 12 years to invent an 85-character alphabet so easy to learn that within a year after its approval by the Cherokee tribal council, the New Testament of the Bible was translated into Cherokee. After the Cherokee removal to Oklahoma in 1838, the alphabet played a critical role in maintaining ties between the new western band of the Cherokee Nation and the remnant of the tribe remaining in the East.

Traveler's Rest

Children love the miniature Traveler's Rest on the porch of the original.

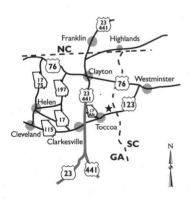

Restrooms
Handicapped Access

This impressive crossroads inn was built in 1815 and later enlarged to accommodate a steady stream of settlers heading into the new frontier and native american territory.

On your tour, you'll see the original square-bottomed nails that roof the building still in place, a child's cradle carved from a solid black walnut log, cider and wine presses in the basement kitchen, looms used by slaves to weave linen and cotton cloth, and the secret drawers in the fireplace mantle where the inn's owner, Devereaux Jarrett, kept his gold nuggets. The rest of the grounds includes a dairy house, a wellhouse, a meathouse, and a slave cabin.

LOCATION
Off US 123, six miles east of Toccoa.
706-886-2256
www.ngeorgia.com/parks/travelers.html

SEASON
Thursday–Saturday, 9 am – 5 pm;
Sunday, 2:00–5:30 pm.

TIME ALLOWANCE
1 hour

COST
Adults: $2.50
Children 6–12: $1.50
Under 6: free

BRING ALONG
Questions, camera, a sweater or jacket on cool days—the inn is unheated.

NOTE
Compare the small boulder covered with pictographs in the back yard to the carvings found on the stones at Track Rock (p.106).

EVOLUTION OF A PLANTATION

The inn at Traveler's Rest began as a private home in 1815. Its evolution over the next 37 years into a thriving plantation with a tanyard, cotton gin, blacksmith, grist mill, post office, sawmill, tavern, country store, gold mine, ferry service, and resting spot for weary travelers had everything to do with its location at the end of a wide new road—the Unicoi Turnpike—linking Maryville, Tennessee, and the Tugaloo River in Georgia. Within a year of its completion, the turnpike had become a major north-south artery to the frontier.

THE INN HOSTED FAMOUS VISITORS

The turnpike brought a number of historical figures to north Georgia and Traveler's Rest. John C. Calhoun, the noted politician, stayed here, and today's visitors to the inn will see the room where Joseph E. Brown, governor and senator from Georgia, is said to have spent his wedding night.

AN ISLAND OF LUXURY ON A ROUGH AND READY ROAD

Traveling the turnpike was a rough and ready adventure, and the inn was considered luxurious. It was the only building for miles around with glass windows. Still, the average turnpike traveler who stayed there

The Unicoi Turnpike and Traveler's Rest

shared a bed with a stranger for 25¢ a night. According to an Englishman who visited in 1836, a breakfast of "coffee, ham, chicken, good bread and butter, good honey, and plenty of new milk" could be had for another quarter of a dollar.

Because it stood on the edge of wilderness, Traveler's Rest had to be self-sufficient. It produced food, clothing, and necessary goods and

services not only for its owner, but for other businesses and individuals as well. Devereaux Jarrett, who owned Traveler's Rest in its heyday, was one of the wealthiest men in Georgia when he died in 1852. There were two and a half *tons* of pork hanging in the meathouse!

THE DECLINE OF THE INN

As the fortunes of Traveler's Rest rose with the turnpike, so did they eventually decline. By the 1860s, although the Tugaloo River was still a major shipping route, John Calhoun's railroad was carrying most of the passenger traffic. The Civil War and the freeing of the slaves further reduced its productivity and income. It became a state historic site in 1955.

Civil War History

The events and battles of the American Civil War shaped the future of no other state quite like they did Georgia. General William T. Sherman's storming and burning of Atlanta severed the cord of supplies to the Confederate Army fighting in the north. His famous and devastating "March to the Sea" demolished the vital supplies themselves, demoralized the Southern people, and literally split the Confederacy. He could have accomplished none of this without first surviving a number of major battles in the north Georgia mountains.

A PERFECT NATURAL ADVENTURE AND HISTORY LESSON ALL IN ONE

Traveling to these battle sites is the perfect natural adventure and history lesson all in one. Throughout the battlefields are walking and hiking trails, picnic areas, and short auto tours. To really get the feel of the battle, you'll spend the majority of the time outside—along the streams, in the woods, and in the fields where the soldiers of the past fought and suffered. You may even decide to take in one of the reenactments, where the realities of that war are brought to life.

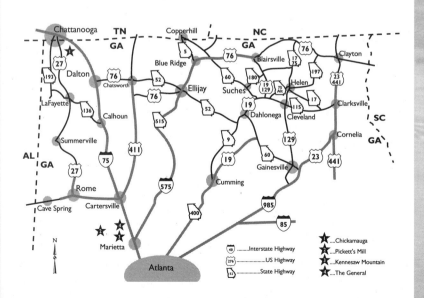

Chickamauga National Battlefield Park

The view is great from the top of the Wilder Brigade monument.

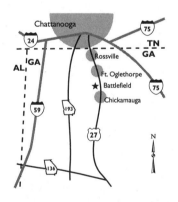

Museum
Restrooms
Picnic Tables
Handicapped Access

he Battle of Chickamauga, fought near the banks of Chickamauga Creek south of Chattanooga, Tennessee, was as bloody as any battle of the Civil War. Here clashed the two major forces west of the Appalachians—the Union Army of the Cumberland led by Major General William Rosecrans and the Confederate Army of Tennessee led by General Braxton Bragg. The battlefield today is maintained much the same as it was in 1863. Monuments and cannons represent and mark the tactical maneuvers of each side, while a variety of interpretive signs and audio boxes explain the battle. Begin at the visitor center, where you'll find exhibits and audio-visual programs explaining the battle and its place in the Civil War.

LOCATION
On US 27 south of Chattanooga, Tennessee, between Chickamauga and Fort Oglethorpe.

SEASON
Year–round.
Daily, 9 am – 5 pm (closed Christmas Day).

TIME ALLOWANCE
2–4 hours

COST
Free. Audio headsets can be rented from the visitor center for a small fee.

BRING ALONG
Camera, Civil war history books, picnic.

NOTE
The visitor center houses an excellent bookstore, with volumes covering the entire Civil War.

CONFEDERATES RETREAT TO GEORGIA

Prior to the Battle of Chickamauga, the Confederate forces (the Army of Tennessee) led by General Braxton Bragg had been in a gradual retreat south all the way from Nashville. In pursuit was the Army of the Cumberland (the Federals) led by Major General William Starke Rosecrans. Rosecrans had defeated Bragg at Stones River near Murfreesboro, Tennessee, on January 3, 1863. Bragg retreated slowly to Chattanooga. Then on September 7, 1863, he again retreated south.

A MAJOR BATTLE UNFOLDS

Chattanooga was a vital link in a major artery of supply lines for the Confederacy. The Federals' plan was to surprise the Confederates by crossing the mountains and entering Chattanooga from the south. Their forces were split into several divisions in order to cross the rough terrain. Rosecrans was delighted to find that with Bragg's retreat, they were able to take the city virtually uncontested. But a number of his divisions were left in vulnerable positions as they crossed Lookout Mountain farther to the south. Bragg recognized this, halted his retreat, and went on the offensive.

BUNGLED ORDERS RULE

Bragg knew he must attack or Chattanooga and the Confederate supply lines to the north would be lost. Early in the morning on

A Brief Story of the Battle

September 18, 1863, the Battle of Chickamauga began. It raged for three days, with both sides suffering heavy losses. Confusion and bungled orders ruled. Orders were given and never received, troops showed up unexpectedly in odd places, and positions were gained only to be lost again due to shortages in ammunition or reinforcements.

CONFEDERATES WIN FIGHT AND DON'T EVEN KNOW IT

During the heavy fighting that occurred that bloody Sunday, September 20, Bragg issued a peremptory order based upon inadequate information. All commands were to advance, regardless of the situation. Despite the misguided order, many of the Union forces fled, and Rosecrans called for an all-out retreat to Chattanooga.

In the chaos, a number of Federals held tight on Snodgrass Hill, which the Confederates attacked repeatedly. Finally at dusk, a unit stumbled onto the remaining Federal forces, only to find that most of them had retreated. The Confederates went to bed that night ready to face another day of battle, but when they awoke, they realized they were alone on the battlefield. All told, the Confederates lost 17,000 men, while the Federals lost 16,000. Bragg had won at Chickamauga, but Rosecrans still held all-important Chattanooga.

Pickett's Mill Battlefield

Artillery, riflery, and hand-to-hand combat served the day during the Battle at Pickett's Mill.

When the Union Army attacked at Pickett's Mill in May 1864, they found dense piney woods and rough terrain. You will find it much the same today, as this is one of the best preserved battlefields in the US. There are no monuments, lines of cannons, or stone effigies as there are at many sites, nor is it crisscrossed with paved roads. To see the battlefield you'll take one of three walking trails. A pamphlet describes the old trenches, mill ruins, and the steep ravine known as the "Hell Hole," where most of the fighting occurred. There is also an indoor interpretive center.

LOCATION
The battlefield is located 5 miles northeast of Dallas on Tabor Church Road.
770-443-7850

SEASON
Year-round. Tuesday–Saturday, 9 am – 5 pm; Sunday, noon – 5 pm.
Closed Monday, Thanksgiving, Christmas, and New Year's Day.

TIME ALLOWANCE
2–3 hours

COST
Adults: $2; children 6–18: $1 (under 6, free).

BRING ALONG
Camera, questions, walking shoes, Civil War history books, picnic, water bottle.

NOTE
Of the three trails—the White (½ mile), the Blue (1½ miles), and the Red (2 miles)—the Blue is the best choice to see the most of the battlefield. The trails have steep, rough sections. Pickett's Mill is very close to *The General* (p. 117) and Kennesaw Mountain (p. 116).

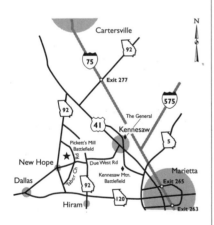

Museum
Restrooms
Picnic Tables

ARE THOSE THE GHOSTS OF CIVIL WAR SOLDIERS?

If you travel to enough Civil War battlefields, sooner or later you're bound to spot what you might think are ghosts—a group of soldiers looking like they just stepped out of the year 1863. These folks are known as reenactors, and they take their jobs seriously.

A REENACTOR TAKES ON A SOLDIER'S IDENTITY

Civil War reenactors come from all walks of life. They could be anybody on the street, but on the battlefield they have taken on the identities of soldiers. Reenactors study as much as possible of their chosen identities. They have learned in which battles their soldiers fought, in which regiment they served, what they

Reenactments — Living History

wore, what they ate, and what kind of rifle they used. During the reenactment, they become those people.

REENACTORS ARE A HARDY BUNCH

Talk to any reenactor and you'll learn more about the Civil War than you ever learned in school. Reenactments come in all forms, from encampments to full-on battles. If a battle was fought in the winter, the reenactment is held then as well. Stories abound of reenactors nearly freezing to death just as their personas did over a hundred years ago, sleeping out on the battlefield with no shelter and only the bodies of other reenactors to keep them warm. During battle reenactments, rifles and cannons fire blanks, but they sound like the real thing. But, unlike the soldiers whose identities they take on for the day, the reenactors can go home after the battle, sleep in a warm bed, and return to another life.

NOTEWORTHY

Major reenactments occur at Resaca in late May, at Tunnel Hill in early September, and at Pickett's Mill in late May or early June of each year. The best source for when and where is the *Camp Chase Gazette*. 740-373-1565 or www.cybergate.net/civilwar/.

Kennesaw Mountain Battlefield Park

After heavy losses, the Union troops prevailed at Kennesaw.

Museum
Restrooms
Picnic Tables
Handicapped Access

For General William T. Sherman, Kennesaw Mountain was the last mountain between him and Atlanta. His ultimate "March to the Sea" split the Confederacy and produced rancor that lasted in the South for generations. This national battlefield park covers a large tract of land just west of Marietta. You can see the major points on a self-guided auto tour or get intimate with the battle from one of the hiking trails, which range from two to sixteen miles in length. A highlight is to go to the top of Kennesaw Mountain itself, where the cannons still face north and you can view the Atlanta skyline 20 miles to the south. There is a great 20-minute film at the interpretive center as well as other memorabilia.

LOCATION
On Old US 41 between Marietta and Kennesaw. From I-75, take the Ernest Barrett Parkway exit (#263) and follow the signs.

SEASON
Year-round. Closed Christmas Day.

TIME ALLOWANCE
Two hours to all day if you take a long hike.

COST
Free

BRING ALONG
Camera, questions, hiking shoes, Civil War history books, water bottle.

NOTE
Just down the road in Kennesaw is the famous locomotive, *The General* (see next page), and nearby is Pickett's Mill Battlefield (p. 114).

UNION SPIES PLOT TO CUT SUPPLY LINES

A visit to Big Shanty (Kennesaw) means you'll see the old rail engine *The General*, and therein lies a story. One year after the attack on Fort Sumter, which began the War Between the States, a group of Union spies plotted to destroy the rail line between Chattanooga and Atlanta. If successful, they would cut off the main supply line that fed and clothed the Confederate Army.

THE GENERAL IS STOLEN WHILE CREW EATS BREAKFAST

James Andrews and his raiders boarded the train pulled by *The General* in Marietta at 4 am on April 12, 1862. When the train stopped for breakfast, they took control and steamed away, leaving the crew behind. Their plan was to move north and destroy track, bridges, and tunnels along the way. The crew of *The General* had a different idea. Conductor William Fuller and his staff took the theft as a personal affront. They followed the raiders for two miles on foot before they procured a platform handcar and, later, a train. The chase was on as Fuller pursued *The General* from station to station by any means he could.

SUPPLY LINES UNBROKEN

Finally, in Adairsville, Fuller hopped a southbound engine, *The Texas*, and began the pursuit at top speed—in

The Great Railway Chase

reverse! Andrews and his raiders did everything they could to slow or stop their pursuers—including releasing a burning rail car in their path—but to no avail. Just before Ringgold Gap, *The General* ran out of steam. The raiders' mission had failed, and the supply line to the gray army was unbroken. *The General* survived the chase—and the war—and continued service on the Western & Atlantic and the Louisville & Nashville for another 30 years.

VISIT THE GENERAL

The General is now housed in the Kennesaw Civil War Museum in downtown Kennesaw (formerly Big Shanty), only steps away from where it was apprehended in 1862. To get there from Kennesaw Mountain, follow Old US 41 into Kennesaw and turn right on Cherokee Street.

Classic Attractions

All across the top of Georgia you'll see countless attractions to tempt your purse. Many are the type that could be found just about anywhere and are really not natural adventures as we describe them at all. There are, however, a select number of attractions we call "Classic" that you won't want to miss.

THESE ATTRACTIONS YOU DO NOT WANT TO MISS

The discovery of gold near Dahlonega in 1828 was the first event to bring folks into northern Georgia in large numbers. There is still gold in "them thar hills," and you can learn how the early prospectors panned for it at one of the original mines. Atop Springer Mountain is the southern terminus of the Appalachian Trail. The "AT" has become so famous that it is an attraction all on its own. It's fun just to set foot on it, and you'll get excited every time you see a highway sign saying it crosses ahead. Burt's Pumpkin Farm is something else. The vast number of those big bright orange pumpkins is amazing. You'll beam from ear to ear while tramping through the orange sea. And don't forget the festivals that celebrate the seasons of north Georgia. At these, locals share their mountain traditions and you can take home a sampling of what this part of the state is all about.

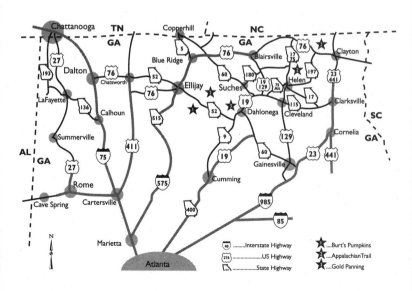

Gold Panning

It won't be long until you are plucking out flakes of real gold.

hroughout north Georgia you'll find a number of locations to pan for gold, and the best are just outside Dahlonega. If these seem like just another attraction to grab the tourist dollar, you should know that most are the real McCoy, situated on the sites of original mines. There is still a lot of gold in the Georgia hills, and if you want to learn how the miners of old found their riches, a commercial gold mine is the best place to begin. It's an inexpensive activity that's also a lot of fun. And who knows—there's always the chance you'll strike it rich!

LOCATION
There are two mines in the Dahlonega area:
- **Crisson Gold Mine** is located on US 19 just north of Dahlonega. 706-864-6363.
- **Consolidated Gold Mine** is located at the junction of US 19, GA 60, and GA 52, just down from the main square and adjacent to the Wal-mart parking area. 706-864-8473.

SEASON
Year-round, seven days a week.

TIME ALLOWANCE
Allow at least an hour. You may want to stay a half or full day.

COST
Prices start at around $2.50 for a plate of sand (good for about 20 minutes).

BRING ALONG
Camera, glass vial (to store your gold—you can buy them at the mine), extra clothes for kids (they'll get wet).

NOTE
Plan a stop at the gold museum in Dahlonega before you head out to pan so the old mining structures will make more sense (p. 76).

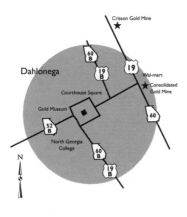

Restrooms

Panning for Gold

YOU, TOO, CAN PAN FOR GOLD

People have been panning for gold for well over a hundred years now, and the process has not changed one bit. To watch, it seems rather simple. Take a metal pan that looks like a pie plate, scoop up some sand from the bottom of a stream and slosh it around, then pick out the gold. In reality, it's not quite so easy as it first appears, but with just a little practice, you too can become a gold panner.

YOU NEED A GOOD PAN

First of all, you need a good pan. It should be about 10 inches in diameter and sturdy. One of a dull metal color works best. Anything new and shiny-looking will just compete with the shininess of the gold. If it's too flimsy, it won't support the weight of the sand.

THE MORE YOU FIND MAKES FINDING MORE EASIER

Whether you're at a commercial operation or on a local stream, the process is the same. Scoop up a plateful of sand and dip it in the water. Now gently slosh it around, keeping the plate fairly level. Once most of the water is sloshed out, tip the plate up and scoop off about a third of the sand from the top side. Add more water and repeat. Continue until the majority of the sand and larger bits of gravel are gone from the pan. Gold is heavier than everything else and will naturally move to the bottom.

Look for the shiny flecks of yellow metal in the fine sand that remains in the plate.

REAL GOLD VERSUS FOOL'S GOLD

Are you a fool or a real miner? Fool's gold is iron pyrite. It looks a lot like gold to the beginner and actually fools you into thinking you've got more than you really do. What's the difference? It's mostly in the color, but also in the weight. As you know, iron is pretty heavy stuff too, so iron pyrite sinks to the bottom of your pan along with the real gold. Gold is heavier, but you can never tell that from just a few flakes. The real telltale sign is the color. Real gold is the color of … well … gold! Iron pyrite is gold-colored too, but side by side, it looks more silvery and a bit sparkly. No matter what you actually find, the real fun is in the search. And if you find it hard to leave, check your temperature. You may just have a touch of "gold fever."

Appalachian Trail

Take in the view from Springer Mountain, the southern terminus of the Appalachian Trail.

Stretching over 2,100 miles and spanning 14 states, this most famous footpath has its southern terminus in north Georgia. Quite a few folks hike the entire length of the Appalachian Trail (AT) each year. These rugged individuals are known as "through-hikers." If you have only a few hours (instead of several months), a shorter hike on the trail can be very rewarding. Several good walks on the AT are accessible in this region. The trail is well marked with signs and white blazes.

LOCATION
The Appalachian Trail crosses roadways at a number of places in north Georgia. See pp. 128–129 for access points.

SEASON
Year–round

TIME ALLOWANCE
As long as you like.

COST
Free

BRING ALONG
Comfortable walking clothing, sturdy shoes, camera, sun protection, water bottle.

NOTE
The AT can provide a good break to stretch your legs during an auto tour. Just watch for the familiar green "Appalachian Trail Ahead" sign.

THE AT BEGINS (OR ENDS) IN NORTH GEORGIA

North Georgia has the distinction of being home to the southern terminus of the Appalachian Trail. This white-blazed footpath leads from the top of Springer Mountain over 2,100 miles to the top of Mount Katahdin in Maine. In Georgia, the route covers 77.5 of those miles. For the through-hikers heading north, the Georgia mountains are their proving grounds.

HIGH POINT OF THE GEORGIA APPALACHIAN TRAIL

Along those first miles are quite a few points of interest. The route crosses the tops of 30 mountains and passes through 31 gaps. Going

Plaques like this are found bolted to rocks at numerous sites.

The Appalachian Trail in Georgia

from gap to mountaintop usually means a pretty major climb. Along the way are 13 rustic shelters where hikers may spend the night. The trail passes alongside or through four wilderness areas—Raven Cliffs, Mark Trail, Tray Mountain, and Southern Nantahala. The highest point is atop Blood Mountain at 4,461 feet, and all along the way are rocky precipices affording stunning views of the surrounding Blue Ridge. Hikers get their water from small streams or springs, many of which are located just off the trail. Blue-blazed trails always lead to water.

UNCOMMON EXPERIENCES ON THE NORTH GEORGIA APPALACHIAN TRAIL

Hikers along the Appalachian Trail in Georgia may have some experiences rather uncommon elsewhere on the trail. From Milepost 8 to around Milepost 16 the trail passes above Army Ranger Camp Frank Merrill. It's not unusual to run into Rangers out on maneuvers. They'll be the ones in full camouflage and carrying rifles. At Milepost 30.6, the trail passes through Neels Gap and crosses US 19/129. Here, an outfitter shop, Mountain Crossings at Walasi-Yi Center (706-745-6095), straddles the trail. Hikers must pass through the building to continue on their path.

Burt's Pumpkin Farm

Pumpkins (some of them huge!) spread out in all directions.

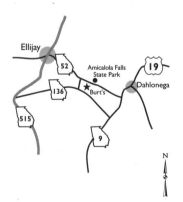

Restrooms
Picnic Tables
Handicapped Access
Entertainment

ant to see the most, the biggest, and the largest variety of pumpkins all at once? In the fall, head for Burt's Pumpkin Farm. Get anywhere near the place and you can't miss it. Row after row of the hugest and most orange of orange pumpkins line up in the field selection area. It literally looks like a sea of pumpkins, and every variety is available for sale, along with gourds, winter squash, and farm-raised popcorn. It's a great place to get your jack-o'-lantern or pick up some items for fall arrangements. Collect them in your own wheelbarrow, provided by Burt's.

LOCATION
On GA 52 between Ellijay and Dahlonega and just west of the entrance to Amicalola Falls State Park. Call 800-600-BURT.

SEASON
September through early November

TIME ALLOWANCE
1–2 hours

COST
Admission is free. Pumpkins range in price from 50¢ to over $50 each.

BRING ALONG
Camera, walking shoes, money for pumpkins and other treats.

NOTE
Burt's also offers hayrides at certain times on the weekends and puts on a rather dazzling light show during the Christmas season.

A TRADITION THAT'S OVER 2,000 YEARS OLD

It all started with the Celts in what is now Great Britain, Ireland, and northern France more than 2,000 years ago. The Celtic new year began on November 1, and on the night preceding it they honored Samhain, the Celtic lord of death. This marked the beginning of the season of cold, darkness, and decay. The Celts believed that Samhain allowed the souls of the dead to return to their earthly homes for the night. During the celebration, people wore costumes made from animal heads and skins.

HALLOWEEN AND TRICK OR TREATING

Over the years, the customs of the descendents of these Celts changed somewhat in different regions. For Christians, November 1 became All Saints Day, and November 2 became All Souls Day. The mass that was said on All Saints Day was called Allhallowmas. The evening before became known as All Hallow e'en, or Halloween. In Ireland, on October 31 people begged for food in a parade to honor the god Muck Olla. In England, families sat by the fire and told stories while they ate apples and nuts. The next day, poor people went a-souling (begging). People in Scotland paraded through fields and villages, carrying torches.

Origin of the Jack-o'-Lantern

PUMPKINS BECOME JACK-O'-LANTERNS

Many of the people parading about in England and Ireland in those days started hollowing out beets, potatoes, and turnips to use as lanterns on Halloween. According to Irish legend, there was a miser named Jack, who, when he died, could not enter heaven because of his stingy practices. He could not enter hell either, because he had played tricks on the devil. As a result, Jack had to walk the earth with his lantern until Judgement Day. The Irish called their hollowed out vegetable lanterns *jack-o'-lanterns*. When the tradition made its way to America, pumpkins began to be used instead.

Festivals & Special Events

Cloggers are a common sight at mountain festivals.

hroughout the seasons there are many special events worth attending if you happen to be in the area. You can count on finding something going on Memorial Day, the Fourth of July, or Labor Day in just about any of the local communities. A lot of the fun is "discovering" an event on your own. Keep a keen eye on the newspapers and an open ear to the radio. You'll soon be venturing out to who knows where.

LOCATION
Almost every town and community has one or more special events throughout the year. See pp. 129–130 for a list of "extra special" local events and festivals.

SEASON
April–October

TIME ALLOWANCE
Half day

COST RANGE
Most are free, but you'll want pocket money for food and crafts.

BRING ALONG
Camera, good walking shoes.

Face painting is always popular.

Mountain Music

THE BEST PLACE TO HEAR MOUNTAIN MUSIC IS AT A FESTIVAL

Some people call it folk music. Some people call it country music. Others call it bluegrass. But the people who know what they are talking about call it "mountain music," and the best place to hear mountain music is at a north Georgia festival. If there's not a live band playing, then there's taped music blasting out through the crowds. Without it, the festival just wouldn't be festive.

GO IT ALONE OR PLAY WITH A GROUP

Mountain music involves strings and lots of them—on fiddles, guitars, banjos, dulcimers, bass fiddles, and more. Anything that can twang will do. People play mouth harps, jugs, and sometimes even saws, and although singing is not essential, it sure sounds nice and rounds out a band. Some people prefer to perform solo, while others join a larger group.

OLD TIME MOUNTAIN MUSIC COMES FROM WAY BACK

People have been playing mountain music in north Georgia ever since white settlers arrived here. As folks moved into the mountains, they brought their instruments with them or they made them later on. Almost every homestead had an instrument or two, and folks liked to get together and do what we today call "picking and grinning." Instruments were handed down from generation to generation, as were the tunes. Today, we call this passed-down mountain music "old timey music," and there are bands that specialize in nothing but.

MOUNTAIN MUSIC SURVIVES BY BEING PLAYED

You can learn to play mountain music, but those who are born into it play it best. Those with young ears just seem to pick things up better than those with old ones. If you go down to your local music store and ask for some sheets of mountain music, you won't get very much, if anything. Most of the music has never been put down on paper, and there may be many, many different ways to play the same song. The way this music survives is by being played, and folks learn it by listening to others. In fact, many mountain musicians can't even read music—they play by ear. So if you really want to learn what it is all about, head to a festival in the north Georgia mountains. You'll come home with remnants of the music ringing in your ears.

Appendix

Look for the rectangular white blazes and AT symbol at these locations.

AMICALOLA FALLS STATE PARK/SPRINGER MOUNTAIN

Most folks beginning a through-hike on the AT start at Amicalola Falls State Park on GA 52 between Ellijay and Dahlonega. The lead-in trail is 8.3 miles long to the southern terminus of the AT atop Springer Mountain.

FOREST SERVICE ROUTE 42

The trail crosses FS 42 at four locations: Stover Creek at AT milepost 2.5, Hightower Gap at AT milepost 8.1, Cooper Gap at AT milepost 11.6 and Gooch Gap at AT milepost 16.4.

THREE FORKS

This popular day-hike area is accessed from Forest Service Route 58 and is located at AT milepost 4.1.

WOODY GAP

The AT crosses GA 60 here just south of Suches.

NEELS GAP

The trail crosses US 19/129 between Dahlonega and Blairsville.

HOG PEN AND TESNATEE GAPS

The trail crosses GA 348 at Hog Pen Gap and passes beside GA 348 at Tesnatee Gap north of Helen.

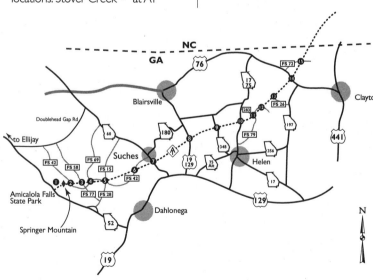

UNICOI GAP [10]
The AT crosses GA 17/75 here north of Helen.

INDIAN GRAVE GAP [11]
Take Forest Service Route 283 off GA 17/75 two miles north of Unicoi Gap to the AT.

TRAY GAP [12]
Take Forest Service Route 79, which is just north of Helen on GA 17/75, to the AT.

ADDIS GAP [13]
Take Forest Service Route 26 off GA 197 adjacent to Lake Burton to the AT.

DICKS CREEK GAP [14]
The AT crosses US 76 here west of Clayton.

BLUE RIDGE GAP [15]
Take Forest Service Route 72 off US 76 just west of Dicks Creek Gap to the AT.

BACKPACKING JUMPING-OFF POINTS

Great trail maps can be purchased from the US Forest Service. See p. 132.

THE COHUTTA WILDERNESS
Located in north-central Georgia on the Tennessee line north of Ellijay, east of US 411, and west of Blue Ridge. There are close to 100 miles of well-marked hiking trails. All trailheads are located on Forest Service dirt roads. Refer to USFS Cohutta Wilderness map for detailed trail routes and directions.

APPALACHIAN TRAIL
Just over 75 miles of the trail are in Georgia. Popular access points are Amicalola Falls State Park, Woody Gap, Neels Gap, Hog Pen Gap, Unicoi Gap, and Dicks Creek Gap. See previous section for details.

LEN FOOTE HIKE INN
Leave the sleeping bag and tent at home and sleep in a real bed after a five-mile backpack to the lodge in Amicalola Falls State Park. Fee includes dinner, breakfast, and a private room. 800-864-7275.

FORT MOUNTAIN STATE PARK
Hike the 8+-mile Gahuti Trail—it makes for a great afternoon hike, overnight sleep-out, or morning hike excursion. The trail circles the top of Fort Mountain. You'll find the trailhead at the Cool Springs Overlook within the park.

CHATTOOGA RIVER TRAIL
Just over 37 miles long, the Chattooga River Trail begins on the Georgia side of the US 76 bridge over the Chattooga. From the bridge, it heads upstream on one side of the river or the other all the way to Ellicott Rock, where South Carolina, North Carolina and Georgia all meet.

FESTIVAL INFORMATION

TALLULAH FALLS WHITEWATER FESTIVAL
1st weekend in April
Crafts, outdoor marketplace, music, watch kayakers paddle Tallulah Gorge. Tallulah Falls Special Events Committee
PO Box 94
Tallulah Falls, GA 30573
706-754-4318
www.georgiamountains.com

(Festival Information continued)

HELEN–ATLANTIC HOT AIR BALLOON RACE AND FESTIVAL

First weekend in June
Music, food, crafts, hot air balloon rides.
Helen Welcome Center
PO Box 730
Helen, GA 30545
www.HelenGeorgia.net

BATTLE OF PICKETT'S MILL LIVING HISTORY ENCAMPMENT

Late May or early June
Civil War reenactment.
Pickett's Mill Battlefield
2640 Mt. Tabor Road
Dallas, GA 30132
770-443-7850
www.gastateparks.org

GEORGIA MOUNTAIN FAIR

early August
Crafts, "old ways" demonstrations, pioneer village, music, food.
Admission fee charged.
Georgia Mountain Fair, Inc.
PO Box 444
Hiawassee, GA 30546
706-896-4191
www.georgia-mountain-fair.com

MOUNTAIN MUSIC FESTIVAL

Labor Day weekend
Mountain music of all kinds.
Vogel State Park
7485 Vogel State Park Road
Blairsville, GA 30512
706-745-2628
www.ngeorgia.com/parks/vogel.html

GREAT LOCOMOTIVE CHASE FESTIVAL

First weekend in October
Crafts, music, parade, pageants, and 1800s log town demonstrations.

Nominal fee. On Adairsville historic public square.
Bartow County Convention and Visitors Bureau
PO Box 200397
Cartersville, GA 30120
770-387-1357 or 800-733-2280
www.notatlanta.org

GEORGIA MARBLE FESTIVAL

First weekend in October
Quarry tours, sculpture and arts competition, crafts, food, music, parade, road race.
Pickens County Chamber of Commerce
500 Stegall Drive
Jasper, GA 30143
706-692-5600
www.georgiamarble-mountain.org

GOLD RUSH DAYS

mid-October
Hog calling, liars contests, buckdancing, clogging, tobacco spitting, crafts, gold panning, food, music. Free.
Dahlonega Chamber of Commerce
13 South Park St., Dept. G
Dahlonega, GA 30533
800-231-5433
www.dahlonega.org

GEORGIA APPLE FESTIVAL

mid-October
Crafts, food, music, parade, antique cars, apple tasting. Nominal fee. Held at the Ellijay Fairgrounds.
Ellijay Chamber of Commerce
PO Box 505
Ellijay, GA 30540
706-635-7400
www.gilmerchamber.com

ELACHEE NATURE CENTER

Elachee features three different nature trails. The **Ed Dodd Trail** is about one mile long and showcases a wetland environment. The **Mathis Trail** is also about one mile and takes you through varied habitats. The **Boulevard Trail** is a short ¼-mile walk to an overlook. For directions to Elachee, see p. 20.

CARTER'S LAKE NATURE TRAILS

There are four nature trails at Carter's Lake southwest of Ellijay: the **Tumbling Waters Trail** at Ridgeway Recreation Area (1.2 miles), the **Hidden Pond Trail** at Reregulation Dam Area (0.6 miles), the **Talking Rock Trail** at the Damsite Area (2.6 miles), and the **Carter's Lake Trail** at the Damsite Area (0.2 miles). US Army Corps of Engineers. 706-334-2248.

AMICALOLA WILDLIFE INTERPRETIVE TRAIL

2½ miles long. Located on southern side of GA 53 bridge over the Amicalola River between Tate and Dawsonville. View river rapids as well as mountains. Signs and pamphlet describe human and natural history subjects.

LAUREL RIDGE INTERPRETIVE TRAIL

1½ miles. In Smithgall Woods just outside Helen on GA Alt. 75. Diverse habitat and a variety of flora.

LION'S EYE TRAIL

Short trail for the blind or visually impaired. The trail is at Anna Ruby Falls visitor center just north of Helen. Braille signs interpret various features along Smith Creek.

SOSEBEE COVE TRAIL

½-mile loop trail through Sosebee Cove Natural Area. Located on GA 180 west of Vogel State Park. Rare and beautiful wildflowers, ferns, and rare trees. Look for salamanders in the small stream.

WARWOMAN DELL

Short trail through dense forested area with an abundance of wildflowers. Located on Warwoman Road east of Clayton.

FORT MOUNTAIN STATE PARK

0.7-mile **Big Rock Nature Trail** located across from lake in campground. Rugged and diverse habitat of Fort Mountain. View 400-foot cascade.

VOGEL STATE PARK

0.7-mile **Byron Herbert Reese Nature Trail**. Identify trees and plants as well as ecosystem.

BLACK ROCK MOUNTAIN STATE PARK

0.2-mile **Ada-Hi Falls Trail** leads through deciduous hardwood forest down to overlook platform of falls.

ALL PARKS INFORMATION

800-864-7275
www.gastateparks.org

(Georgia State Parks continued)

AMICALOLA FALLS
240 Amicalola Falls Road
Dawsonville, GA 30534
706-265-4703 or 800-573-9656
www.ngeorgia.com/parks/
amicalola.html

BLACK ROCK MOUNTAIN
PO Drawer A
Mountain City, GA 30562
706-746-2141
www.ngeorgia.com/parks/
blackrock.html

CLOUDLAND CANYON
122 Cloudland Canyon Park Road
Rising Fawn, GA 30738
706-657-4050
www.ngeorgia.com/parks/
cloudland.html

FORT MOUNTAIN
181 Fort Mountain Park Road
Chatsworth, GA 30705
706-695-2621
www.ngeorgia.com/parks/fort.html

JAMES H. "SLOPPY" FLOYD
2800 "Sloppy" Floyd Lake Road
Summerville, GA 30747
706-857-0826
www.ngeorgia.com/parks/sloppy.html

MOCCASIN CREEK
3655 GA Hwy 197
Clarkesville, GA 30523
706-947-3194
www.ngeorgia.com/parks/
moccasin.html

RED TOP MOUNTAIN
781 Red Top Mountain Road
Cartersville, GA 30121
770-975-4226 or 800-573-9658
www.ngeorgia.com/parks/redtop.html

TALLULAH GORGE
PO Box 248
Tallulah Falls, GA 30573
706-754-7970
www.ngeorgia.com/parks/tallulah.html

UNICOI
PO Box 997
Helen, GA 30545
706-878-3982 or 800-573-9659
www.ngeorgia.com/parks/unicoi.html

VOGEL
7485 Vogel State Park Road
Blairsville, GA 30512
706-745-2628
www.ngeorgia.com/parks/vogel.html

CHATTAHOOCHEE NATIONAL FOREST

FOREST SUPERVISOR'S OFFICE
Regional, trail and topographic maps.
1755 Cleveland Hwy.
Gainesville, GA 30501
770-297-3000
www.fs.fed.us/conf/welcome.htm

ARMUCHEE RANGER DISTRICT
806 East Villanow Street
LaFayette, GA 30728
706-638-1085

BRASSTOWN RANGER DISTRICT
PO Box 9
Blairsville, GA 30512
706-745-6928

CHATTOOGA RANGER DISTRICT
200 Highway 197 North
Clarkesville, GA 30523
706-754-6221

COHUTTA RANGER DISTRICT
401 Gil Maddox Parkway
Chatsworth, GA 30705
706-695-6736

TALLULAH RANGER DISTRICT
809 Highway 441 South
Clayton, GA 30525
706-782-3320

TOCCOA RANGER DISTRICT
6050 Appalachian Parkway
Blue Ridge, GA 30513
706-632-3031

CHAMBERS OF COMMERCE

BLUE RIDGE CHAMBER
PO Box 875
Blue Ridge, GA 30513
800-899-6867
www.blueridgemountains.com

CARTERSVILLE CHAMBER
PO Box 200397
Cartersville, GA 30120
800-733-2280
www.notatlanta.org

CHATSWORTH CHAMBER
126 North Third Avenue
Chatsworth, GA 30705
706-695-6060
www.mchamber@northga.net

CLAYTON CHAMBER
PO Box 761
Clayton, GA 30525
706-782-4812
www.gamountains.com/rabun

DALTON CHAMBER
524 Holiday Avenue
Dalton, GA 30720
706-278-7373
www.nwgeorgia.com/
daltonwhitfieldchamber

DAHLONEGA CHAMBER
13 South Park St., Dept. G
Dahlonega, GA 30533
800-231-5543
www.dahlonega.org

ELLIJAY CHAMBER
PO Box 505
Ellijay, GA 30540
706-635-7400
www.gilmerchamber.com

GAINESVILLE CHAMBER
PO Box 374
Gainesville, GA 30403
770-532-6206
www.ghcc.com

HELEN CHAMBER
PO Box 730
Helen, GA 30545
706-878-2521
www.HelenGeorgia.net

JASPER CHAMBER
500 Stegall Drive
Jasper, GA 30143
706-692-5600
www.georgiamarble-mountain.org

LAFAYETTE CHAMBER
PO Box 430
Rock Spring, GA 30739
706-375-7702
www.walkercochamber.com

ROME CHAMBER
1 Riverside Parkway
Rome, GA 30161
706-291-7663
www.romegeorgia.com

NATIONAL FOREST RECREATION AREAS

ANDREWS COVE
Camping, hiking, fishing. On GA 75 north of Cleveland.

ANNA RUBY FALLS
Picnicking, hiking, visitor center. North of Helen adjacent to Unicoi State Park.

DUKES CREEK
Picnicking, hiking, fishing. On Russell/ Brasstown Scenic Byway north of Helen.

LAKE CONASAUGA
Camping, picnicking, hiking, swimming, fishing. On Forest Route 68 north of Fort Mountain State Park.

LAKE WINFIELD SCOTT
Camping, picnicking, hiking, swimming, fishing. East of Suches on GA 180.

DEEP HOLE
Camping, hiking, fishing. Along Toccoa River on GA 60 north of Suches.

COOPER CREEK
Camping, picnicking, hiking, fishing. Off GA 60 north of Suches.

MULKY
Camping, hiking, fishing. Off GA 60 north of Suches.

CHESTATEE OVERLOOK
Picnicking. On GA 60 south of Suches.

DOCKERY LAKE
Camping, picnicking, fishing, hiking. Off GA 60 south of Suches.

FRANK GROSS
Camping, fishing. Adjacent to fish hatchery off GA 60 north of Suches.

DESOTO FALLS
Camping, picnicking, hiking, fishing. On US 19/129 north of Dahlonega.

WATERS CREEK
Camping, picnicking, hiking, fishing. Off US 19 north of Dahlonega.

WOODY GAP
Picnicking, hiking. On GA 60 south of Suches.

TALLULAH RIVER
Camping, hiking, fishing. Off US 76 west of Clayton.

TATE BRANCH
Camping, fishing, hiking. Off US 76 west of Clayton.

SANDY BOTTOM
Camping, fishing. Off US 76 west of Clayton.

POPCORN OVERLOOK
Picnicking. On US 76 west of Clayton.

KEOWN FALLS
Picnicking, hiking. On Pocket Road east of Villanow.

THE POCKET
Camping, hiking, picnicking. On Pocket Road east of Villanow.

LAKE BLUE RIDGE
Camping, picnicking, hiking, boating. South of Blue Ridge off Aska Road.

PANTHER CREEK
Picnicking, hiking. Off Old US 441 north of Cornelia.

LAKE CHATUGE
Camping, boating, fishing, hiking. Off US 76 west of Hiawassee.

LAKE RUSSELL
Camping, picnicking, swimming, fishing, hiking. Off Dicks Hill Parkway east of Cornelia.

MORGANTON POINT

Camping, picnicking, hiking, swimming, boating, fishing. Off GA 60 south of Morganton.

RABUN BEACH

Camping, picnicking, hiking, boating, fishing. Off US 441 south of Clayton.

WARWOMAN DELL

Picnicking, nature trail. On Warwoman Road east of Clayton.

REGIONAL GUIDEBOOKS & SUGGESTED READING

AUTO TOURING

TOURING THE BACKROADS OF NORTH AND SOUTH GEORGIA

by Victoria and Frank Logue
John F. Blair Publisher, 1997

WATERFALL WALKS & DRIVES IN GA, AL & TN

by Mark Morrison
HF Publishing, 1995

BICYCLING

OFF THE BEATEN TRACK: VOLUME 3—A GUIDE TO MOUNTAIN BIKING IN NORTH GEORGIA, 3RD ED.

by Jim Parham
Milestone Press, 1999

ROAD BIKE NORTH GEORGIA

by Jim Parham
Milestone Press, 1998

HIKING

THE HIKING TRAILS OF NORTH GEORGIA, 3RD ED.

by Tim Homan
Peachtree Publishers, 1997

FLY FISHING

TROUT FISHING IN NORTH GEORGIA

by Jimmy Jacobs
Peachtree Publishers, 1997

LEAVES AND FLOWERS

FALL COLOR FINDER

by Ritchie Bell & Anne Lindsey
Laurel Hill Press, 1991

GREAT SMOKY MOUNTAINS WILDFLOWERS

by Campbell, Hudson & Sharp
Univ. of Tennessee Press, 1977
Written for the Smokies, but works the best of what we've seen for N. GA.

PADDLESPORTS

SOUTHEASTERN WHITEWATER

by Monte Smith
Pahsimeroi Press, 1995

SUGGESTED READING

TRAIL OF TEARS, THE RISE AND FALL OF THE CHEROKEE NATION

by John Ehle
Anchor Books, 1988

THE CIVIL WAR IN GEORGIA: AN ILLUSTRATED TRAVELER'S GUIDE

by Richard Lenz
Lenz Design and Communications, Inc., 1995

SHARING NATURE WITH CHILDREN

by Joseph Cornell
Dawn Publications, 1979

There are hundreds of miles of hiking trails to choose from in north Georgia. We recommend you consult a hiking guidebook before you set out, but here are a few suggestions to get you started.

SPRINGER MOUNTAIN/ THREE FORKS

You can do one of two loops here, or combine them for a figure-8 hike. To get there, see p. 128.

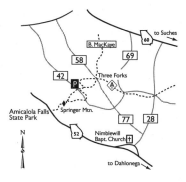

THREE FORKS LOOP

Total distance: 4.1 miles.
The trailhead is located on Forest Service Route 42 northeast of Amicalola Falls State Park. It's the #2 access point to the Appalachian Trail on the map on page 128. From the trailhead parking lot, first hike north on the AT (white blaze), then on the combined AT/Benton MacKaye Trail. When the AT splits off to the left, take it and follow down alongside Stover Creek to Three Forks. At Three Forks, turn right on the Benton MacKaye Trail (white diamond blaze). Follow it up the mountain to where you'll retrace your steps to back to the trailhead.

SPRINGER MOUNTAIN

Total distance: 4.5 miles. Start from the same trailhead as the Three Forks hike. Follow the AT (white blaze) south and ascend Springer Mountain. Pass the left turn to the Benton MacKaye Trail and continue all the way to the top, where there will be a plaque commemorating the southern terminus of the Appalachian Trail. Retrace your steps back to the Benton MacKaye Trail (white diamond blaze), turn right, and follow it all the way back to the trailhead parking area.

BLOOD MOUNTAIN/ VOGEL STATE PARK

There are several options. Try these for starters.

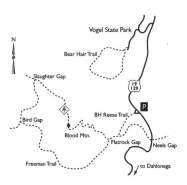

BLOOD MOUNTAIN UP & BACK

Total Distance: 4.8 miles.
This is one of the most popular hikes on the AT in Georgia. Start at Neels Gap hiker parking lot on US 19/129. Climb Blood Mountain by going south on first the Byron Herbert Reece Trail and then the AT to the old stone shelter. Return the same way. The trail is steep and rocky, and the view is fantastic from the top.

BLOOD MOUNTAIN LOOP

Total distance: 7 miles.
Start at Neels Gap as in the Blood Mountain Up & Back hike. At Flatrock Gap turn left on the Freeman Trail. Rejoin the AT at Bird Gap and turn right. Hike to Slaughter Gap, turn right, and then return over top of Blood Mountain.

BEAR HAIR TRAIL

Total distance: 4 miles.
The trail is in Vogel State Park just off US 19/129. You'll find the trailhead by bearing left past the visitor center and following the signs. It is a loop hike of moderate difficulty and can be done in either direction. Just follow the orange blazes.

CLOUDLAND CANYON STATE PARK

To get there, see p. 88.

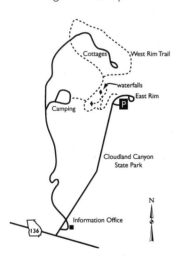

WATERFALL TRAIL

Total distance: approximately 1 mile. This short hike takes you down to have a look at two waterfalls on Daniel Creek. It's downhill to the falls and uphill to return. You'll pass interesting rock formations along the way. The trail starts at the canyon overlook in Cloudland Canyon State Park.

WEST RIM LOOP TRAIL

Total distance: 5 miles.
Parts of this trail follow along the west rim of Cloudland Canyon, with side trails out to wooden platform overlooks. You can start in the campground or by taking the Waterfall Trail down through the upper canyon.

BLACK ROCK MOUNTAIN STATE PARK

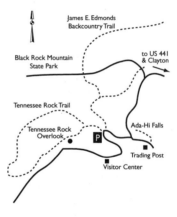

TENNESSEE ROCK TRAIL

Total distance: 2.2 miles.
You'll pass the trailhead on your right as you head for the park visitor center. This is a beautiful hike, following a loop that eventually takes you over the summit of Black Rock Mountain and on to the Tennessee Rock Overlook. Make sure to walk the loop counterclockwise.

CANOEING

MOUNTAIN OUTDOOR EXPEDITIONS
Lower Cartecay River Road
Ellijay, GA 30540
706-635-2524

APPALACHIAN OUTFITTERS
Hwy. 60 South
Dahlonega, GA 30533
706-864-7117 or 800-426-7117

THE WILDWOOD OUTPOST
Hwy. 384
Helen, GA 30545
706-865-4451 or 800-553-2715

BICYCLING

CARTECAY BICYCLE SHOP
52 North Main Street
Ellijay, GA 30540
706-635-BIKE or 888-276-2453

MOUNTAIN ADVENTURES CYCLERY
52 Clayton Drive
Dahlonega, GA 30533
706-864-8525

WOODY'S MOUNTAIN BIKES
Hwy. 356
Helen, GA 30545
706-878-3715

TUBING

COOL RIVER TUBING CO.
Helen, GA 30545
706-878-COOL

ALPINE TUBING
Helen, GA 30545
706-878-8823

GARDEN TUBING
Helen, GA 30545
706-878-3472

GEORGIA MOUNTAIN TUBING
Helen, GA 30545
706-878-1919

WHITEWATER RAFTING (CHATTOOGA RIVER)

SOUTHEASTERN EXPEDITIONS
US 76
Clayton, GA 30525
706-782-4331 or 800-868-7238

NANTAHALA OUTDOOR CENTER
Chattooga Ridge Road
Mountain Rest, SC 29664
800-232-7238

WILDWATER LTD.
Academy Road
Long Creek, SC 29658
800-451-9972

OFF-PAVEMENT DRIVING ROUTES

COHUTTAS DRIVE
There are several options for an entry point for a drive through the Cohuttas. From the west, start in Eton, Crandall, or Cisco. From the south, work your way in off GA 52 from Ellijay, and from the east, head in off GA 5 above Blue Ridge. To see the most you'll want to end up on Forest Service Routes 64, 68,

and 17. Just about any way you do it, this is an all-day affair. And make sure you have a full tank of gas going in. It does not get much more backwoods than this.

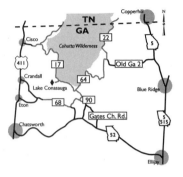

SIXTEEN GAP DRIVE

Like in the Cohuttas, you can enter into this area from just about any direction. Your goal is to end up on Forest Service Route 42. Much of this road parallels the Appalachian Trail. Once on top of the high ridges, you'll hop from gap to gap (16 in all if you go the whole distance of FS 42) with spectacular views from both sides of the road.

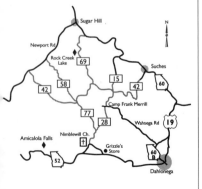

COOPER CREEK/ DUNCAN RIDGE DRIVE

This route surrounds the Cooper Creek Scenic Area and traverses Duncan Ridge. You can access the roads from several points, but a nice place to start is Lake Winfield Scott. You'll enjoy the diversity from ridgetop to streamside bottomland.

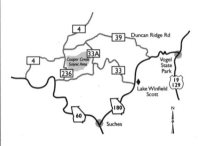

UPPER HOOCH/ HIGH SHOALS DRIVE

This route just north of Helen is bisected by GA 17/75, giving you the option of following the Upper Chattahoochee River almost from its source near Unicoi Gap on Forest Service Route 44, or heading up and over the Tennessee Divide to High Shoals Falls. You can combine the two for a good day's outing.

Index

Milestone Press
Outdoor Adventure Guides

OFF THE BEATEN TRACK MOUNTAIN BIKE GUIDE SERIES
by Jim Parham

Volume I: Western North Carolina—The Smokies

Volume II: Western North Carolina—Pisgah

Volume III: North Georgia

Volume IV: East Tennessee

Volume V: Northern Virginia

Volume VI: West Virginia—Northern Highlands

Tsali Mountain Bike Trails Map

Bull Mountain Mtn Bike Trails Map

ROAD BIKE SERIES

Road Bike Asheville, NC: Favorite Rides of the Blue Ridge Bicycle Club
by The Blue Ridge Bicycle Club

Road Bike the Smokies: 16 Great Rides in North Carolina's Great Smoky Mountains
by Jim Parham

Road Bike North Georgia: 25 Great Rides in the Mountains and Valleys of North Georgia
by Jim Parham

PLAYBOATING

A Playboater's Guide to the Ocoee River
by Kelly Fischer

Playboating the Nantahala River: An Entry Level Guide
by Kelly Fischer

ADVENTURING

Natural Adventures in the Mountains of Western North Carolina
by Mary Ellen Hammond and Jim Parham

A NOTE TO THE READER:
Can't find the Milestone Press book you want at a bookseller, bike shop, or outfitter store near you? Don't despair—you can order it directly from us. Write: Milestone Press, PO Box 158, Almond, NC 28702; call us at 828-488-6601; or shop online at http://www.milestonepress.com.

We welcome your comments and suggestions regarding the contents of this book. Please write us at the address above or e-mail us at: nang@milestonepress.com.